Alexander the Great

By

Jacob Abbott

Cover Photograph: Andrew Dunn

ISBN: 978-1-78139-165-5

Contents

List of Illustrations

PREFACE

THE history of the life of every individual who has, for any reason, attracted extensively the attention of mankind, has been written in a great variety of ways by a multitude of authors, and persons sometimes wonder why we should have so many different accounts of the same thing. The reason is, that each one of these accounts is intended for a different set of readers, who read with ideas and purposes widely dissimilar from each other. Among the twenty millions of people in the United States, there are perhaps two millions, between the ages of fifteen and twenty-five, who wish to become acquainted, in general, with the leading events in the history of the Old World, and of ancient times, but who, coming upon the stage in this land and at this period, have ideas and conceptions so widely different from those of other nations and of other times, that a mere republication of existing accounts is not what they require. The story must be told expressly to them. The things that are to be explained, the points that are to be brought out, the comparative degree of prominence to be given to the various particulars, will all be different, on account of the difference in the situation, the ideas, and the objects of these new readers, compared with those of the various other classes of readers which former authors have had in view. It is for this reason, and with this view, that the present series of historical narratives is presented to the public. The author, having had some opportunity to become acquainted with the position, the ideas, and the intellectual wants of those whom he addresses, presents the result of his labors to them, with the hope that it may be found successful in accomplishing its design.

HIS CHILDHOOD AND YOUTH

Notwithstanding the briefness of Alexander's career, he ran through, during that short period, a very brilliant series of exploits, which were so bold, so romantic, and which led him into such adventures in scenes of the greatest magnificence and splendor, that all the world looked on with astonishment then, and mankind have continued to read the story since, from age to age, with the greatest interest and attention.

The secret of Alexander's success was his character. He possessed a certain combination of mental and personal attractions, which in every age gives to those who exhibit it a mysterious and almost unbounded ascendency over all within their influence. Alexander was characterized by these qualities in a very remarkable degree. He was finely formed in person, and very prepossessing in his manners. He was active, athletic, and full of ardor and enthusiasm in all that he did. At the same time, he was calm, collected, and considerate in emergencies requiring caution, and thoughtful and far-seeing in respect to the bearings and consequences of his acts. He formed strong attachments, was grateful for kindnesses shown to him, considerate in respect to the feelings of all who were connected with him in any way, faithful to his friends, and generous toward his foes. In a word, he had a noble character, though he devoted its energies unfortunately to conquest and war. He lived, in fact, in an age when great personal and mental powers had scarcely any other field for their exercise than this. He entered upon his career with great ardor, and the position in which he was placed gave him the opportunity to act in it with prodigious effect.

There were several circumstances combined, in the situation in which Alexander was placed, to afford him a great opportunity for the exercise of his vast powers. His native country was on the confines of Europe and Asia. Now Europe and Asia were, in those days, as now, marked and distinguished by two vast masses of social and civilized life, widely dissimilar from each other. The Asiatic side was occupied by the Persians, the Medes, and the Assyrians. The European side by the Greeks and Romans. They were separated from each other by the waters of the Hellespont, the Ægean Sea, and the Mediterranean, as will be seen by the map. These waters constituted a sort of natural barrier, which kept the two races apart. The races formed, accordingly, two vast organizations, distinct and widely different from each other, and of course rivals and enemies.

It is hard to say whether the Asiatic or European civilization was the highest. The two were so different that it is difficult to compare them. On the Asiatic side there was wealth, luxury, and splendor; on the European, energy, genius, and force. On the one hand were vast cities, splendid palaces, and gardens which were the wonder of the world; on the other, strong citadels, military roads and bridges, and compact and well-defended towns. The Persians had enormous armies, perfectly provided for, with beautiful tents, horses elegantly caparisoned, arms and munitions of war of the finest workmanship, and officers magnificently dressed, and accustomed to a life of luxury and splendor. The Greeks and Romans, on the other hand, prided themselves on their compact bodies of troops, inured to hardship and thoroughly disciplined. Their officers gloried not in luxury and parade, but in the courage, the steadiness, and implicit obedience of their troops, and in their own science, skill, and powers of military calculation. Thus there was a great difference in the whole system of social and military organization in these two quarters of the globe.

Now Alexander was born the heir to the throne of one of the Grecian kingdoms. He possessed, in a very remarkable degree, the energy, and enterprise, and military skill so characteristic of the Greeks and Romans. He organized armies, crossed the boundary between Europe and Asia, and spent the twelve years of his career in a most triumphant military incursion into the very center of the seat of Asiatic power, destroying the Asiatic armies, conquering the most splendid cities, defeating or taking captive the kings, and princes, and generals that opposed his progress. The whole world looked on with wonder to see such a course of conquest, pursued so successfully by so young a man, and with so small an army, gaining continual victories, as it did, over such vast numbers of foes, and making conquests of such accumulated treasures of wealth and splendor.

The name of Alexander's father was Philip. The kingdom over which he reigned was called Macedon. Macedon was in the northern part of Greece. It was a kingdom about twice as large as the State of Massachusetts, and one third as large as the State of New York. The name of Alexander's mother was Olympias. She was the daughter of the King of Epirus, which was a kingdom somewhat smaller than Macedon, and lying westward of it. Both Macedon and Epirus will be found upon the map at the commencement of this volume. Olympias was a woman of very strong and determined character. Alexander seemed to inherent her energy, though in his case it was combined with other qualities of a more attractive character, which his mother did not possess.

He was, of course, as the young prince, a very important personage in his father's court. Every one knew that at his father's death he would become King of Macedon, and he was consequently the object of a great deal of care and attention. As he gradually advanced in the years of his boyhood, it was observed by all who knew him that he was endued with extraordinary qualities of mind and of character, which seemed to indicate, at a very early age, his future greatness.

Although he was a prince, he was not brought up in habits of luxury and effeminacy. This would have been contrary to all the ideas which were entertained by the Greeks in those days. They had then no fire-arms, so that in battle the combatants could not stand quietly, as they can now, at a distance from the enemy, coolly discharging musketry or cannon. In ancient battles the soldiers rushed toward each other, and fought hand to hand, in close combat, with swords, or spears, or other weapons requiring great personal strength, so that headlong bravery and muscular force were the qualities which generally carried the day.

The duties of officers, too, on the field of battle, were very different then from what they are now. An officer *now* must be calm, collected, and quiet. His business is to plan, to calculate, to direct, and arrange. He has to do this sometimes, it is true, in circumstances of the most imminent danger, so that he must be a man of great self-possession and of undaunted courage. But there is very little occasion for him to exert any great physical force.

In ancient times, however, the great business of the officers, certainly in all the subordinate grades, was to lead on the men, and set them an example by performing themselves deeds in which their own great personal prowess was displayed. Of course it was considered extremely important that the child destined to be a general should become robust and powerful in constitution from his earliest years, and that he should be inured to hardship and fatigue. In the early part of Alexander's life this was the main object of attention.

The name of the nurse who had charge of our hero in his infancy was Lannice. She did all in her power to give strength and hardihood to his constitution, while, at the same time, she treated him with kindness and gentleness. Alexander acquired a strong affection for her, and he treated her with great consideration as long as he lived. He had a governor, also, in his early years, named Leonnatus, who had the general charge of his education. As soon as he was old enough to learn, they appointed him a preceptor also, to teach him such branches as were generally taught to young princes in those days. The name of this preceptor was Lysimachus.

They had then no printed books, but there were a few writings on parchment rolls which young scholars were taught to read. Some of these writings were treatises on philosophy, others were romantic histories, narrating the exploits of the heroes of those days—of course, with much exaggeration and embellishment. There were also some poems, still more romantic than the histories, though generally on the same themes. The greatest productions of this kind were the writings of Homer, an ancient poet who lived and wrote four or five hundred years before Alexander's day. The young Alexander was greatly delighted with Homer's tales. These tales are narrations of the exploits and adventures of certain great warriors at the siege of Troy—a siege which lasted ten years—and they are written with so much beauty and force, they contain such admirable delineations of character, and such graphic and vivid descriptions of romantic adventures, and picturesque and striking scenes, that they have been admired in every age by all who have learned to understand the language in which they are written.

Alexander could understand them very easily, as they were written in his mother tongue. He was greatly excited by the narrations themselves, and pleased with the flowing smoothness of the verse in which the tales were told. In the latter part of his course of education he was placed under the charge of Aristotle, who was one of the most eminent philosophers of ancient times. Aristotle had a beautiful copy of Homer's poems prepared expressly for Alexander, taking great pains to have it transcribed with perfect correctness, and in the most elegant manner. Alexander carried this copy with him in all his campaigns. Some years afterward, when he was obtaining conquests over the Persians, he took, among the spoils of one of his victories, a very beautiful and costly casket, which King Darius had used for his jewel-

4

ry or for some other rich treasures. Alexander determined to make use of this box as a depository for his beautiful copy of Homer, and he always carried it with him, thus protected, in all his subsequent campaigns.

Alexander was full of energy and spirit, but he was, at the same time, like all who ever become truly great, of a reflective and considerate turn of mind. He was very fond of the studies which Aristotle led him to pursue, although they were of a very abstruse and difficult character. He made great progress in metaphysical philosophy and mathematics, by which means his powers of calculation and his judgment were greatly improved.

He early evinced a great degree of ambition. His father Philip was a powerful warrior, and made many conquests in various parts of Greece, though he did not cross into Asia. When news of Philip's victories came into Macedon, all the rest of the court would be filled with rejoicing and delight; but Alexander, on such occasions, looked thoughtful and disappointed, and complained that his father would conquer every country, and leave him nothing to do.

At one time some embassadors from the Persian court arrived in Macedon when Philip was away These embassadors saw Alexander, of course, and had opportunities to converse with him. They expected that he would be interested in hearing about the splendors, and pomp, and parade of the Persian monarchy. They had stories to tell him about the famous hanging gardens, which were artificially constructed in the most magnificent manner, on arches raised high in the air; and about a vine made of gold, with all sorts of precious stones upon it instead of fruit, which was wrought as an ornament over the throne on which the King of Persia often gave audience; of the splendid palaces and vast cities of the Persians; and the banquets, and fêtes, and magnificent entertainments and celebrations which they used to have there. They found, however, to their surprise, that Alexander was not interested in hearing about any of these things. He would always turn the conversation from them to inquire about the geographical position of the different Persian countries, the various routes leading into the interior, the organization of the Asiatic armies, their system of military tactics, and, especially, the character and habits of Artaxerxes, the Persian king.

The embassadors were very much surprised at such evidences of maturity of mind, and of far-seeing and reflective powers on the part of the young prince. They could not help comparing him with Artaxerxes. "Alexander," said they, "is *great*, while our king is only *rich*."

The truth of the judgment which these embassadors thus formed in respect to the qualities of the young Macedonian, compared with those held in highest estimation on the Asiatic side, was fully confirmed in the subsequent stages of Alexander's career.

In fact, this combination of a calm and calculating thoughtfulness, with the ardor and energy which formed the basis of his character, was one great secret of Alexander's success. The story of Bucephalus, his famous horse, illustrates this in a very striking manner. This animal was a war-horse of very spirited character, which had been sent as a present to Philip while Alexander was young. They took the horse out into one of the parks connected with the palace, and the king, together with many of his courtiers, went out to view him. The horse pranced about in a very furious manner, and seemed entirely unmanageable. No one dared to mount him. Philip, instead of being gratified at the present, was rather disposed to be displeased that they had sent him an animal of so fiery and apparently vicious a nature that nobody dared to attempt to subdue him.

In the mean time, while all the other by-standers were joining in the general condemnation of the horse, Alexander stood quietly by, watching his motions, and attentively studying his character. He perceived that a part of the difficulty was caused by the agitations which the horse experienced in so strange and new a scene, and that he appeared, also, to be somewhat frightened by his own shadow, which happened at that time to be thrown very strongly and distinctly upon the ground. He saw other indications, also, that the high excitement which the horse felt was not viciousness, but the excess of noble and generous impulses. It was courage, ardor, and the consciousness of great nervous and muscular power.

Philip had decided that the horse was useless, and had given orders to have him sent back to Thessaly, whence he came. Alexander was very much concerned at the prospect of losing so fine an animal. He begged his father to allow him to make the experiment of mounting him. Philip at first refused, thinking it very presumptuous for such a youth to attempt to subdue an animal so vicious that all his experienced horsemen and grooms condemned him; however, he at length consented. Alexander went up to the horse and took hold of his bridle. He patted him upon the neck, and soothed him with his voice, showing, at the same time, by his easy and unconcerned manner, that he was not in the least afraid of him. A spirited horse knows immediately when any one approaches him in a timid or cautious manner. He appears to look with contempt on such a master, and to determine not to

6

submit to him. On the contrary, horses seem to love to yield obedience to man, when the individual who exacts the obedience possesses those qualities of coolness and courage which their instincts enable them to appreciate.

ALEXANDER AND BUCEPHALUS

At any rate, Bucephalus was calmed and subdued by the presence of Alexander. He allowed himself to be caressed. Alexander turned his head in such a direction as to prevent his seeing his shadow. He quietly and gently laid off a sort of cloak which he wore, and sprang upon the horse's back. Then, instead of attempting to restrain him, and worrying and checking him by useless efforts to hold him in, he gave him the rein freely, and animated and encouraged him with his voice, so that the horse flew across the plains at the top of his speed, the king and the courtiers looking on, at first with fear and trembling, but soon afterward with feelings of the greatest admiration and pleasure. After the horse had satisfied himself with his run it was easy to rein him in, and Alexander returned with him in safety to the king. The courtiers overwhelmed him with their praises and congratulations. Philip commended him very highly: he told him that he deserved a larger kingdom than Macedon to govern.

Alexander's judgment of the true character of the horse proved to be correct. He became very tractable and docile, yielding a ready submission to his master in every thing. He would kneel upon his fore legs at Alexander's command, in order that he might mount more easily. Alexander retained him for a long time, and made him his favorite war horse. A great many stories are related by the historians of those days of his sagacity and his feats of war. Whenever he was equipped for the field with his military trappings, he seemed to be highly elated with pride and pleasure, and at such times he would not allow any one but Alexander to mount him.

What became of him at last is not certainly known. There are two accounts of his end. One is, that on a certain occasion Alexander got carried too far into the midst of his enemies, on a battle field, and that, after fighting desperately for some time, Bucephalus made the most extreme exertions to carry him away. He was severely wounded again and again, and though his strength was nearly gone, he would not stop, but pressed forward till he had carried his master away to a place of safety, and that then he hopped down exhausted, and died. It may be, however, that he did not actually die at this time, but slowly recovered; for some historians relate that he lived to be thirty years old—which is quite an old age for a horse—and that he then died. Alexander caused him to be buried with great ceremony, and built a small city upon the spot in honor of his memory. The name of this city was Bucephalia.

Alexander's character matured rapidly, and he began very early to act the part of a man. When he was only sixteen years of age, his father, Philip, made him regent of Macedon while he was absent on a great military campaign among the other states of Greece. Without doubt Alexander had, in this regency, the counsel and aid of high officers of state of great experience and ability. He acted, however, himself, in this high position, with great energy and with complete success; and, at the same time, with all that modesty of deportment, and that delicate consideration for the officers under him—who, though inferior in rank, were yet his superiors in age and experience—which his position rendered proper, but which few persons so young as he would have manifested in circumstances so well calculated to awaken the feelings of vanity and elation.

Afterward, when Alexander was about eighteen years old, his father took him with him on a campaign toward the south, during which Philip fought one of his great battles at Chæronea, in Bœotia. In the arrangements for this battle, Philip gave the command of one of the wings of the army to Alexander, while he reserved the other for himself. He felt some solicitude in giving his young son so important a charge, but he endeavored to guard against the danger of an unfortunate result by putting the ablest generals on Alexander's side, while he reserved those on whom he could place less reliance for his own. Thus organized, the army went into battle.

Philip soon ceased to feel any solicitude for Alexander's part of the duty. Boy as he was, the young prince acted with the utmost bravery, coolness, and discretion. The wing which he commanded was victorious, and Philip was obliged to urge himself and the officers with him to greater exertions, to avoid being outdone by his son. In the end Philip was completely victorious, and the result of this great battle was to make his power paramount and supreme over all the states of Greece.

Notwithstanding, however, the extraordinary discretion and wisdom which characterized the mind of Alexander in his early years, he was often haughty and headstrong, and in cases where his pride or his resentment were aroused, he was sometimes found very impetuous and uncontrollable. His mother Olympias was of a haughty and imperious temper, and she quarreled with her husband, King Philip; or, perhaps, it ought rather to be said that he quarreled with her. Each is said to have been unfaithful to the other, and, after a bitter contention, Philip repudiated his wife and married another lady. Among the festivities held on the occasion of this marriage, there was a great banquet, at which Alexander was present, and an incident occurred which strikingly illustrates the impetuosity of his character.

One of the guests at this banquet, in saying something complimentary to the new queen, made use of expressions which Alexander considered as in disparagement of the character of his mother and of his own birth. His anger was immediately aroused. He threw the cup from which he had been drinking at the offender's head. Attalus, for this was his name, threw, his cup at Alexander in return; the guests at the table where they were sitting rose, and a scene of uproar and confusion ensued.

Philip, incensed at such an interruption of the order and harmony of the wedding feast, drew his sword and rushed toward Alexander, but by some accident he stumbled and fell upon the floor. Alexander looked upon his fallen father with contempt and scorn, and exclaimed, "What a fine hero the states of Greece have to lead their armies—a man that can not get across the floor without tumbling down." He then turned away and left the palace. Immediately afterward he joined his mother Olympias, and went away with her to her native country, Epirus, where the mother and son remained for a time in a state of open quarrel with the husband and father.

In the mean time Philip had been planning a great expedition into Asia. He had arranged the affairs of his own kingdom, and had formed a strong combination among the states of Greece by which powerful armies had been raised, and he had been designated to command them.

His mind was very intently engaged in this vast enterprise. He was in the flower of his years, and at the height of his power. His own kingdom was in a very prosperous and thriving condition, and his ascend-ascendency over the other kingdoms and states on the European side had been fully established. He was excited with ambition, and full of hope. He was proud of his son Alexander, and was relying upon his efficient aid in his schemes of conquest and aggrandizement. He had married a youthful and beautiful bride, and was surrounded by scenes of festivity, congratulation, and rejoicing. He was looking forward to a very brilliant career considering all the deeds that he had done and all the glory which he had acquired as only the introduction and prelude to the far more distinguished and conspicuous part which he was intending to perform.

Alexander, in the mean time, ardent and impetuous, and eager for glory as he was, looked upon the position and prospects of his father with some envy and jealousy. He was impatient to be monarch himself. His taking sides so promptly with his mother in the domestic quarrel was partly owing to the feeling that his father was a hindrance and an obstacle in the way of his own greatness and fame. He felt within himself powers and capacities qualifying him to take his father's place, and reap for himself the harvest of glory and power which seemed to await the Grecian armies in the coming campaign. While his father lived, however, he could be only a prince; influential, accomplished, and popular, it is true, but still without any substantial and independent power. He was restless and uneasy at the thought that, as his father was in the prime and vigor of manhood, many long years must elapse before he could emerge from this confined and subordinate condition. His restlessness and uneasiness were, however, suddenly ended by a very extraordinary occurrence, which called him, with scarcely an hour's notice, to take his father's place upon the throne.

BEGINNING OF HIS REIGN

ALEXANDER was suddenly called upon to succeed his father on the Macedonian throne, in the most unexpected manner, and in the midst of scenes of the greatest excitement and agitation. The circumstances were these:

Philip had felt very desirous, before setting out upon his great expedition into Asia, to become reconciled to Alexander and Olympias. He wished for Alexander's co-operation in his plans; and then, besides, it would be dangerous to go away from his own dominions with such a son left behind, in a state of resentment and hostility.

So Philip sent kind and conciliatory messages to Olympias and Alexander, who had gone, it will be recollected, to Epirus, where *her* friends resided. The brother of Olympias was King of Epirus. He had been at first incensed at the indignity which had been put upon his sister by Philip's treatment of her; but Philip now tried to appease his anger, also, by friendly negotiations and messages. At last he arranged a marriage between this King of Epirus and one of his own daughters, and this completed the reconciliation. Olympias and Alexander returned to Macedon, and great preparations were made for a very splendid wedding.

Philip wished to make this wedding not merely the means of confirming his reconciliation with his former wife and son, and establishing friendly relations with the King of Epirus: he also prized it as an occasion for paying marked and honorable attention to the princes and great generals of the other states of Greece. He consequently made his preparations on a very extended and sumptuous scale, and sent invitations to the influential and prominent men far and near.

These great men, on the other hand, and all the other public authorities in the various Grecian states, sent compliments, congratulations, and presents to Philip, each seeming ambitious to contribute his share to the splendor of the celebration. They were not wholly disinterested in this, it is true. As Philip had been made commander-in-chief of the Grecian armies which were about to undertake the conquest of Asia, and as, of course, his influence and power in all that related to that vast enterprise would be paramount and supreme; and as all were ambitious to have a large share in the glory of that expedition, and to participate, as much as possible, in the power and in the renown which seemed to be at Philip's disposal, all were, of course, very anxious to secure his favor. A short time before, they were contending against him; but now, since he had established his ascendency, they all eagerly joined in the work of magnifying it and making it illustrious.

Nor could Philip justly complain of the hollowness and falseness of these professions of friendship. The compliments and favors which he offered to them were equally hollow and heartless. He wished to secure *their* favor as a means of aiding him up the steep path to fame and power which he was attempting to climb. They wished for his, in order that he might, as he ascended himself, help them up with him. There was, however, the greatest appearance of cordial and devoted friendship. Some cities sent him presents of golden crowns, beautifully wrought, and of high cost. Others dispatched embassies, expressing their good wishes for him, and their confidence in the success of his plans. Athens, the city which was the great seat of literature and science in Greece sent a *poem*, in which the history of the expedition into Persia was given by anticipation. In this poem Philip was, of course, triumphantly successful in his enterprise. He conducted his armies in safety through the most dangerous passes and defiles; he fought glorious battles, gained magnificent victories, and possessed himself of all the treasures of Asiatic wealth and power. It ought to be stated, however, in justice to the poet, that, in narrating these imaginary exploits, he had sufficient delicacy to represent Philip and the Persian monarch by fictitious names.

The wedding was at length celebrated, in one of the cities of Macedon, with great pomp and splendor. There were games, and shows, and military and civic spectacles of all kinds to amuse the thousands of spectators that assembled to witness them. In one of these spectacles they had a procession of statues of the gods. There were twelve of these statues, sculptured with great art, and they were borne along on elevated pedestals, with censers, and incense, and various ceremonies of homage, while vast multitudes of spectators lined the way. There was a thirteenth statue, more magnificent than the other twelve, which represented Philip himself in the character of a god.

This was not, however, so impious as it would at first view seem, for the gods whom the ancients worshiped were, in fact, only deification, of old heroes and kings who had lived in early times, and had acquired a reputation for supernatural powers by the fame of their exploits, exaggerated in descending by tradition in superstitious times. The ignorant multitude accordingly, in those days, looked up to a living king with almost the same reverence and homage which they felt for their deified heroes; and these deified heroes furnished them with all the ideas they had of God. Making a monarch a god, therefore, was no very extravagant flattery.

After the procession of the statues passed along, there came bodies of troops, with trumpets sounding and banners flying. The officers rode on horses elegantly caparisoned, and prancing proudly. These troops escorted princes, ambassadors, generals, and great officers of state, all gorgeously decked in their robes, and wearing their badges and insignia.

At length King Philip himself appeared in the procession. He had arranged to have a large space left, in the middle of which he was to walk. This was done in order to make his position the more conspicuous, and to mark more strongly his own high distinction above all the other potentates present on the occasion. Guards preceded and followed him, though at considerable distance, as has been already said. He was himself clothed with white robes, and his head was adorned with a splendid crown.

The procession was moving toward a great theater, where certain games and spectacles were to be exhibited. The statues of the gods were to be taken into the theater, and placed in conspicuous positions there, in the view of the assembly, and then the procession itself was to follow. All the statues had entered except that of Philip, which was just at the door, and Philip himself was advancing in the midst of the space left for him, up the avenue by which the theater was approached, when an occurrence took place by which the whole character of the scene, the destiny of Alexander, and the fate of fifty nations, was suddenly and totally changed. It was this. An officer of the guards, who had his position in the procession near the king, was seen advancing impetuously toward him, through the space which separated him from the rest, and, before the spectators had time even to wonder what he was going to do, he stabbed him to the heart. Philip fell down in the street and died.

A scene of indescribable tumult and confusion ensued. The murderer was immediately cut to pieces by the other guards. They found, however, before he was dead, that it was Pausanias, a man of high standing and influence, a general officer of the guards. He had had horses provided, and other assistance ready, to enable him to make his escape, but he was cut down by the guards before he could avail himself of them.

An officer of state immediately hastened to Alexander, and announced to him his father's death and his own accession to the throne. An assembly of the leading counselors and statesmen was called, in a hasty and tumultuous manner, and Alexander was proclaimed king with prolonged and general acclamations. Alexander made a speech in reply. The great assembly looked upon his youthful form and face as he arose, and listened with intense interest to hear what he had to say. He was between nineteen and twenty years of age; but, though thus really a boy, he spoke with all the decision and confidence of an energetic man. He said that he should at once assume his father's position, and carry forward his plans. He hoped to do this so efficiently that every thing would go directly onward, just as if his father had continued to live, and that the nation would find that the only change which had taken place was in the *name* of the king.

The motive which induced Pausanias to murder Philip in this manner was never fully ascertained. There were various opinions about it. One was that it was an act of private revenge, occasioned by some neglect or injury which Pausanias had received from Philip. Others thought that the murder was instigated by a party in the states of Greece, who were hostile to Philip, and unwilling that he should command the allied armies that were about to penetrate into Asia. Demosthenes, the celebrated orator, was Philip's great enemy among the Greeks. Many of his most powerful orations were made for the purpose of arousing his countrymen to resist his ambitious plans and to curtail his power. These orations were called his Philippics, and from this origin has arisen the practice, which has prevailed ever since that day, of applying the term philippics to denote, in general, any strongly denunciatory harangues.

Now Demosthenes, it is said, who was at this time in Athens, announced the death of Philip in an Athenian assembly before it was possible that the news could have been conveyed there. He accounted for his early possession of the intelligence by saying it was communicated to him by some of the gods. Many persons have accordingly supposed that the plan of assassinating Philip was devised in Greece;

that Demosthenes was a party to it; that Pausanias was the agent for carrying it into execution; and that Demosthenes was so confident of the success of the plot, and exulted so much in this certainty, that he could not resist the temptation of thus anticipating its announcement.

There were other persons who thought that the *Persians* had plotted and, accomplished this murder, having induced Pausanias to execute the deed by the promise of great rewards. As Pausanias himself, however, had been instantly killed, there was no opportunity of gaining any information from him on the motives of his conduct, even if he would have been disposed to impart any.

At all events, Alexander found himself suddenly elevated to one of the most conspicuous positions in the whole political world. It was not simply that he succeeded to the throne of Macedon; even this would have been a lofty position for so young a man; but Macedon was a very small part of the realm over which Philip had extended his power. The ascendency which he had acquired over the whole Grecian empire, and the vast arrangements he had made for an incursion into Asia, made Alexander the object of universal interest and attention. The question was, whether Alexander should attempt to take his father's place in respect to all this general power, and undertake to sustain and carry on his vast projects, or whether he should content himself with ruling, in quiet, over his native country of Macedon.

Most prudent persons would have advised a young prince, under such circumstances, to have decided upon the latter course. But Alexander had no idea of bounding his ambition by any such limits. He resolved to spring at once completely into his father's seat, and not only to possess himself of the whole of the power which his father had acquired, but to commence, immediately, the most energetic and vigorous efforts for a great extension of it.

His first plan was to punish his father's murderers. He caused the circumstances of the case to be investigated, and the persons suspected of having been connected with Pausanias in the plot to be tried. Although the designs and motives of the murderers could never be fully ascertained, still several persons were found guilty of participating in it, and were condemned to death and publicly executed.

Alexander next decided not to make any change in his father's appointments to the great offices of state, but to let all the departments of public affairs go on in the same hands as before. How sagacious a line of conduct was this! Most ardent and enthusiastic young men, in the circumstances in which he was placed, would have been elated and vain at their elevation, and would have replaced the old and well-tried servants of the father with personal favorites of their own age, inexperienced and incompetent, and as conceited as themselves. Alexander, however, made no such changes, He continued the old officers in command, endeavoring to have every thing go on just as if his father had not died.

There were two officers in particular who were the ministers on whom Philip had mainly relied. Their names were Antipater and Parmenio. Antipater had charge of the civil, and Parmenio of military affairs. Parmenio was a very distinguished general. He was at this time nearly sixty years of age. Alexander had great confidence in his military powers, and felt a strong personal attachment for him. Parmenio entered into the young king's service with great readiness, and accompanied him through almost the whole of his career. It seemed strange to see men of such age, standing, and experience, obeying the orders of such a boy; but there was something in the genius, the power, and the enthusiasm of Alexander's character which inspired ardor in all around him, and made every one eager to join his standard and to aid in the execution of his plans.

Macedon, as will be seen on the following map, was in the northern part of the country occupied by the Greeks, and the most powerful states of the confederacy and all the great and influential cities were south of it. There was Athens, which was magnificently built, its splendid citadel crowning a rocky hill in the center of it. It was the great seat of literature, philosophy, and the arts, and was thus a center of attraction for all the civilized world. There was Corinth, which was distinguished for the gayety and pleasure which reigned there. All possible means of luxury and amusement were concentrated within its walls. The lovers of knowledge and of art, from all parts of the earth, flocked to Athens, while those in pursuit of pleasure, dissipation, and indulgence chose Corinth for their home. Corinth was beautifully situated on the isthmus, with prospects of the sea on either hand. It had been a famous city for a thousand years in Alexander's day.

There was also Thebes. Thebes was farther north than Athens and Corinth. It was situated on an elevated plain, and had, like other ancient cities, a strong citadel, where there was at this time a Macedonian garrison, which Philip had placed there. Thebes was very wealthy and powerful. It had also been celebrated as the birth-place of many poets and philosophers, and other eminent men. Among these was Pindar, a very celebrated poet who had flourished one or two centuries before the time of Alexander. His descendants still lived in

Thebes, and Alexander, some time after this, had occasion to confer upon them a very distinguished honor.

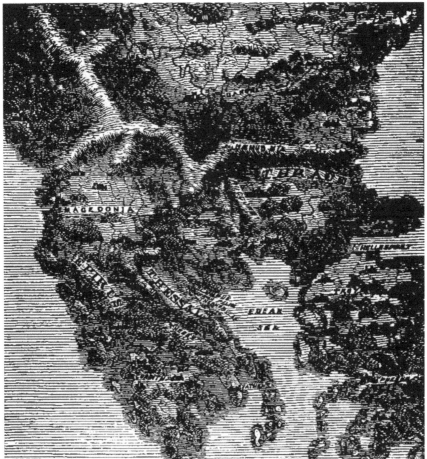

MAP OF MACEDON AND GREECE

There was Sparta also, called sometimes Lacedæmon. The inhabitants of this city were famed for their courage, hardihood, and physical strength, and for the energy with which they devoted themselves to the work of war. They were nearly all soldiers, and all the arrangements of the state and of society, and all the plans of education, were designed to promote military ambition and pride among the officers and fierce and indomitable courage and endurance in the men.

These cities and many others, with the states which were attached to them, formed a large, and flourishing, and very powerful community, extending over all that part of Greece which lay south of Macedon.

Philip, as has been already said, had established his own ascendency over all this region, though it had cost him many perplexing negotiations and some hard fought battles to do it. Alexander considered it somewhat uncertain whether the people of all these states and cities would be disposed to transfer readily, to so youthful a prince as he, the high commission which his father, a very powerful monarch and soldier, had extorted from them with so much difficulty. What should he do in the case? Should he give up the expectation of it? Should he send embassadors to them, presenting his claims to occupy his father's place? Or should he not act at all, but wait quietly at home in Macedon until they should decide the question?

Instead of doing either of these things, Alexander decided on the very bold step of setting out himself, at the head of an army, to march into southern Greece, for the purpose of presenting in person, and, if necessary, of enforcing his claim to the same post of honor and power which had been conferred upon his father. Considering all the circumstances of the case, this was perhaps one of the boldest and most decided steps of Alexander's whole career. Many of his Macedonian advisers counseled him not to make such an attempt; but Alexander would not listen to any such cautions. He collected his forces, and set forth at the head of them.

Between Macedon and the southern states of Greece was a range of lofty and almost impassable mountains. These mountains extended through the whole interior of the country, and the main route leading into southern Greece passed around to the eastward of them, where they terminated in cliffs, leaving a narrow passage between the cliffs and the sea. This pass was called the Pass of Thermopylæ, and it was considered the key to Greece. There was a town named Anthela near the pass, on the outward side.

There was in those days a sort of general congress or assembly of the states of Greece, which was held from time to time, to decide questions and disputes in which the different states were continually getting involved with each other. This assembly was called the Amphictyonic Council, on account, as is said, of its having been established by a certain king named Amphictyon. A meeting of this council was appointed to receive Alexander. It was to be held at Thermopylæ, or, rather, at Anthela, which was just without the pass, and was the usual place at which the council assembled. This was because the pass was in an intermediate position between the northern and southern portions of Greece, and thus equally accessible from either.

In proceeding to the southward, Alexander had first to pass through Thessaly, which was a very powerful state immediately south of Macedon. He met with some show of resistance at first, but not much. The country was impressed with the boldness and decision of character manifested in the taking of such a course by so young a man. Then, too, Alexander, so far as he became personally known, made a very favorable impression upon every one. His manly and athletic form, his frank and open manners, his spirit, his generosity, and a certain air of confidence, independence, and conscious superiority, which were combined, as they always are in the case of true greatness, with an unaffected and unassuming modesty—these and other traits, which were obvious to all who saw him, in the person and character of Alexander, made every one his friend. Common men take pleasure in yielding to the influence and ascendency of one whose spirit they see and feel stands on a higher eminence and wields higher powers than their own. They like a leader. It is true, they must feel confident of his superiority; but when this superiority stands out so clearly and distinctly marked, combined, too, with all the graces and attractions of youth and manly beauty, as it was in the case of Alexander, the minds of men are brought very easily and rapidly under its sway.

The Thessalians gave Alexander a very favorable reception. They expressed a cordial readiness to instate him in the position which his father had occupied. They joined their forces to his, and proceeded southward toward the Pass of Thermopylæ.

Here the great council was held. Alexander took his place in it as a member. Of course, he must have been an object of universal interest and attention. The impression which he made here seems to have been very favorable. After this assembly separated, Alexander proceeded southward, accompanied by his own forces, and tended by the various princes and potentates of Greece, with their attendants and followers. The feelings of exultation and pleasure with which the young king defiled through the Pass of Thermopylæ, thus attended, must have been exciting in the extreme.

The Pass of Thermopylæ was a scene strongly associated with ideas of military glory and renown. It was here that, about a hundred and fifty years before, Leonidas, a Spartan general, with only three hundred soldiers, had attempted to withstand the pressure of an immense Persian force which was at that time invading Greece. He was one of the kings of Sparta, and he had the command, not only of his three hundred Spartans, but also of all the allied forces of the Greeks that had been assembled to repel the Persian invasion. With the help of

19

these allies he withstood the Persian forces for some time, and as the pass was so narrow between the cliffs and the sea, he was enabled to resist them successfully. At length, however, a strong detachment from the immense Persian army contrived to find their way over the mountains and around the pass, so as to establish themselves in a position from which they could come down upon the small Greek army in their rear. Leonidas, perceiving this, ordered all his allies from the other states of Greece to withdraw, leaving himself and his three hundred countrymen alone in the defile.

He did not expect to repel his enemies or to defend the pass. He knew that he must die, and all his brave followers with him, and that the torrent of invaders would pour down through the pass over their bodies. But he considered himself stationed there to defend the passage, and he would not desert his post. When the battle came on he was the first to fall. The soldiers gathered around him and defended his dead body as long as they could. At length, overpowered by the immense numbers of their foes, they were all killed but one man. He made his escape and returned to Sparta. A monument was erected on the spot with this inscription: "Go, traveler, to Sparta, and say that we lie here, on the spot at which we were stationed to defend our country."

Alexander passed through the defile. He advanced to the great cities south of it—to Athens, to Thebes, and to Corinth. Another great assembly of all the monarchs and potentates of Greece was convened in Corinth; and here Alexander attained the object of his ambition, in having the command of the great expedition into Asia conferred upon him. The impression which he made upon those with whom he came into connection by his personal qualities must have been favorable in the extreme. That such a youthful prince should be selected by so powerful a confederation of nations as their leader in such an enterprise as they were about to engage in, indicates a most extraordinary power on his part of acquiring an ascendency over the minds of men, and of impressing all with a sense of his commanding superiority. Alexander returned to Macedon from his expedition to the southward in triumph, and began at once to arrange the affairs of his kingdom, so as to be ready to enter, unembarrassed, upon the great career of conquest which he imagined was before him.

THE REACTION

A branch of this mountain range, called Rhodope, extends southwardly from about the middle of its length, as may be seen by the map. Rhodope separated Macedonia from a large and powerful country, which was occupied by a somewhat rude but warlike race of men. This country was Thrace. Thrace was one great fertile basin or valley, sloping toward the center in every direction, so that all the streams from the mountains, increased by the rains which fell over the whole surface of the ground, flowed together into one river, which meandered through the center of the valley, and flowed out at last into the Ægean Sea. The name of this river was the Hebrus. All this may be seen distinctly upon the map.

The Balkan, or Mount Hæmus, as it was then called, formed the great northern frontier of Macedon and Thrace. From the summits of the range, looking northward, the eye surveyed a vast extent of land, constituting one of the most extensive and fertile valleys on the globe. It was the valley of the Danube. It was inhabited, in those days, by rude tribes whom the Greeks and Romans always designated as barbarians. They were, at any rate, wild and warlike, and, as they had not the art of writing, they have left us no records of their institutions or their history. We know nothing of them, or of the other half-civilized nations that occupied the central parts of Europe in those days, except what their inveterate and perpetual enemies have thought fit to tell us. According to their story, these countries were filled with nations and tribes of a wild and half-savage character, who could be kept in check only by the most vigorous exertion of military power.

Soon after Alexander's return into Macedon, he learned that there were symptoms of revolt among these nations. Philip had subdued them, and established the kind of peace which the Greeks and Romans were accustomed to enforce upon their neighbors. But now, as they had heard that Philip, who had been so terrible a warrior, was no more, and that his son, scarcely out of his teens, had succeeded to the throne, they thought a suitable occasion had arrived to try their strength. Alexander made immediate arrangements for moving northward with his army to settle the question.

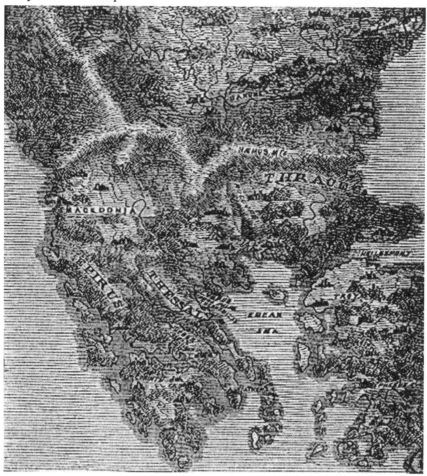

MAP OF MACEDON AND GREECE

He conducted his forces through a part of Thrace without meeting with any serious resistance, and approached the mountains. The soldiers looked upon the rugged precipices and lofty summits before them with awe. These northern mountains were the seat and throne, in the imaginations of the Greeks and Romans, of old Boreas, the hoary god of the north wind. They conceived of him as dwelling among those cold and stormy summits, and making excursions in winter, carrying with him his vast stores of frost and snow, over the southern valleys and plains. He had wings, a long beard, and white locks, all powdered with flakes of snow. Instead of feet, his body terminated in tails of serpents, which, as he flew along, lashed the air, writhing from under his robes. He was violent and impetuous in temper, rejoicing in the devastation of winter, and in all the sublime phenomena of tempests, cold, and snow. The Greek conception of Boreas made an impression upon the human mind that twenty centuries have not been able to efface. The north wind of winter is personified as Boreas to the present day in the literature of every nation of the Western world.

The Thracian forces had assembled in the defiles, with other troops from the northern countries, to arrest Alexander's march, and he had some difficulty in repelling them. They had got, it is said, some sort of loaded wagons upon the summit of an ascent, in the pass of the mountains, up which Alexander's forces would have to march. These wagons were to be run down upon them as they ascended. Alexander ordered his men to advance, notwithstanding this danger. He directed them, where it was practicable, to open to one side and the other, and allow the descending wagon to pass through. When this could not be done, they were to fall down upon the ground when they saw this strange military engine coming, and locking their shields together over their heads, allow the wagon to roll on over them, bracing up energetically against its weight. Notwithstanding these precautions, and the prodigious muscular power with which they were carried into effect, some of the men were crushed. The great body of the army was, however, unharmed; as soon as the force of the wagons was spent, they rushed up the ascent, and attacked their enemies with their pikes. The barbarians fled in all directions, terrified at the force and invulnerability of men whom loaded wagons, rolling over their bodies down a steep descent, could not kill.

Alexander advanced from one conquest like this to another, moving toward the northward and eastward after he had crossed the mountains, until at length he approached the mouths of the Danube. Here one of the great chieftains of the barbarian tribes had taken up his position, with his family and court, and a principal part of his army, upon an island called Peucé, which may be seen upon the map at the beginning of this chapter. This island divided the current of the stream, and Alexander, in attempting to attack it, found that it would be best to endeavor to effect a landing upon the upper point of it.

23

To make this attempt, he collected all the boats and vessels which he could obtain, and embarked his troops in them above, directing them to fall down with the current, and to land upon the island. This plan, however, did not succeed very well; the current was too rapid for the proper management of the boats. The shores, too, were lined with the forces of the enemy, who discharged showers of spears and arrows at the men, and pushed off the boats when they attempted to land. Alexander at length gave up the attempt, and concluded to leave the island, and to cross the river itself further above, and thus carry the war into the very heart of the country.

It is a serious undertaking to get a great body of men and horses across a broad and rapid river, when the people of the country have done all in their power to remove or destroy all possible means of transit, and when hostile bands are on the opposite bank, to embarrass and impede the operations by every mode in their power. Alexander, however, advanced to the undertaking with great resolution. To cross the Danube especially, with a military force, was, in those days, in the estimation of the Greeks and Romans, a very great exploit. The river was so distant, so broad and rapid, and its banks were bordered and defended by such ferocious foes, that to cross its eddying tide, and penetrate into the unknown and unexplored regions beyond, leaving the broad, and deep, and rapid stream to cut off the hopes of retreat, implied the possession of extreme self-reliance, courage, and decision.

Alexander collected all the canoes and boats which he could obtain up and down the river. He built large rafts, attaching to them the skins of beasts sewed together and inflated, to give them buoyancy. When all was ready, they began the transportation of the army in the night, in a place where the enemy had not expected that the attempt would have been made. There were a thousand horses, with their riders, and four thousand foot soldiers, to be conveyed across. It is customary, in such cases, to swim the horses over, leading them by lines, the ends of which are held by men in boats. The men themselves, with all the arms, ammunition, and baggage, had to be carried over in the boats or upon the rafts. Before morning the whole was accomplished.

The army landed in a field of grain. This circumstance, which is casually mentioned by historians, and also the story of the wagons in the passes of Mount Hæmus, proves that these northern nations were not absolute barbarians in the sense in which that term is used at the present day. The arts of cultivation and of construction must have made some progress among them, at any rate; and they proved, by some of their conflicts with Alexander, that they were well-trained and well-disciplined soldiers.

The Macedonians swept down the waving grain with their pikes, to open a way for the advance of the cavalry, and early in the morning Alexander found and attacked the army of his enemies, who were utterly astonished at finding him on their side of the river. As may be easily anticipated, the barbarian army was beaten in the battle that ensued. Their city was taken. The booty was taken back across the Danube to be distributed among the soldiers of the army. The neighboring nations and tribes were overawed and subdued by this exhibition of Alexander's courage and energy. He made satisfactory treaties with them all; took hostages, where necessary, to secure the observance of the treaties, and then recrossed the Danube and set out on his return to Macedon.

He found that it was *time* for him to return. The southern cities and states of Greece had not been unanimous in raising him to the office which his father had held. The Spartans and some others were opposed to him. The party thus opposed were inactive and silent while Alexander was in their country, on his first visit to southern Greece; but after his return they began to contemplate more decisive action, and afterward, when they heard of his having undertaken so desperate an enterprise as going northward with his forces, and actually crossing the Danube, they considered him as so completely out of the way that they grew very courageous, and meditated open rebellion.

The city of Thebes did at length rebel. Philip had conquered this city in former struggles, and had left a Macedonian garrison there in the citadel. The name of the citadel was Cadmeia. The officers of the garrison, supposing that all was secure, left the soldiers in the citadel, and came, themselves, down to the city to reside. Things were in this condition when the rebellion against Alexander's authority broke out. They killed the officers who were in the city, and summoned the garrison to surrender. The garrison refused, and the Thebans besieged it.

This outbreak against Alexander's authority was in a great measure the work of the great orator Demosthenes, who spared no exertions to arouse the southern states of Greece to resist Alexander's dominion. He especially exerted all the powers of his eloquence in Athens in the endeavor to bring over the Athenians to take sides against Alexander.

While things were in this state—the Thebans having understood that Alexander had been killed at the north, and supposing that, at all events, if this report should not be true, he was, without doubt, still far away, involved in contentions with the barbarian nations, from which it was not to be expected that he could be very speedily extricated—the whole city was suddenly thrown into consternation by the report that a large Macedonian army was approaching from the north, with Alexander at its head, and that it was, in fact, close upon them.

It was now, however, too late for the Thebans to repent of what they had done. They were far too deeply impressed with a conviction of the decision and energy of Alexander's character, as manifested in the whole course of his proceedings since he began to reign, and especially by his sudden reappearance among them so soon after this outbreak against his authority, to imagine that there was now any hope for them except in determined and successful resistance. They shut themselves up, therefore, in their city, and prepared to defend themselves to the last extremity.

Alexander advanced, and, passing round the city toward the southern side, established his head-quarters there, so as to cut off effectually all communication with Athens and the southern cities. He then extended his posts all around the place so as to invest it entirely. These preparations made, he paused before he commenced the work of subduing the city, to give the inhabitants an opportunity to submit, if they would, without compelling him to resort to force. The conditions, however, which he imposed were such that the Thebans thought it best to take their chance of resistance. They refused to surrender, and Alexander began to prepare for the onset.

He was very soon ready, and with his characteristic ardor and energy he determined on attempting to carry the city at once by assault. Fortified cities generally require a siege, and sometimes a very long siege, before they can be subdued. The army within, sheltered behind the parapets of the walls, and standing there in a position above that of their assailants, have such great advantages in the contest that a long time often elapses before they can be compelled to surrender. The besiegers have to invest the city on all sides to cut off all supplies of provisions, and then, in those days, they had to construct engines to make a breach somewhere in the walls, through which an assaulting party could attempt to force their way in.

The time for making an assault upon a besieged city depends upon the comparative strength of those within and without, and also, still more, on the ardor and resolution of the besiegers. In warfare, an army, in investing a fortified place, spends ordinarily a considerable time in burrowing their way along in trenches, half under ground, until they get near enough to plant their cannon where the balls can take effect upon some part of the wall. Then some time usually elapses before a breach is made, and the garrison is sufficiently weakened to render an assault advisable. When, however, the time at length arrives, the most bold and desperate portion of the army are designated to lead the attack. Bundles of small branches of trees are provided to fill up ditches with, and ladders for mounting embankments and walls. The city, sometimes, seeing these preparations going on, and convinced that the assault will be successful, surrenders before it is made. When the besieged do thus surrender, they save themselves a vast amount of suffering, for the carrying of a city by assault is perhaps the most horrible scene which the passions and crimes of men ever offer to the view of heaven.

It is horrible, because the soldiers, exasperated to fury by the resistance which they meet with, and by the awful malignity of the passions always excited in the hour of battle, if they succeed, burst suddenly into the precincts of domestic life, and find sometimes thousands of families—mothers, and children, and defenseless maidens—at the mercy of passions excited to phrensy. Soldiers, under such circumstances, can not be restrained, and no imagination can conceive the horrors of the sacking of a city, carried by assault, after a protracted siege. Tigers do not spring upon their prey with greater ferocity than man springs, under such circumstances, to the perpetration of every possible cruelty upon his fellow man. After an ordinary battle upon an open field, the conquerors have only men, armed like themselves, to wreak their vengeance upon. The scene is awful enough, however, here. But in carrying a city by storm, which takes place usually at an unexpected time, and often in the night, the maddened and victorious assaulters suddenly burst into the sacred scenes of domestic peace, and seclusion, and love—the very worst of men, filled with the worst of passions, stimulated by the resistance they have encountered, and licensed by their victory to give all these passions the fullest and most unrestricted gratification. To plunder, burn, destroy, and kill, are the lighter and more harmless of the crimes they perpetrate.

Thebes was carried by assault. Alexander did not wait for the slow operations of a siege. He watched a favorable opportunity, and burst over and through the outer line of fortifications which defended the city. The attempt to do this was very desperate, and the loss of life great; but it was triumphantly successful. The Thebans were driven back toward the inner wall, and began to crowd in, through the gates, into the city, in terrible confusion. The Macedonians were close upon them, and pursuers and pursued, struggling together, and trampling upon and killing each other as they went, flowed in, like a boiling and raging torrent which nothing could resist, through the open arch-way.

It was impossible to close the gates. The whole Macedonian force were soon in full possession of the now defenseless houses, and for many hours screams, and wailings, and cries of horror and despair testified to the awful atrocity of the crimes attendant on the sacking of a city. At length the soldiery were restrained. Order was restored. The army retired to the posts assigned them, and Alexander began to deliberate what he should do with the conquered town.

He determined to destroy it—to offer, once for all, a terrible example of the consequences of rebellion against him. The case was not one, he considered, of the ordinary conquest of a foe. The states of Greece—Thebes with the rest—had once solemnly conferred upon him the authority against which the Thebans had now rebelled. They were *traitors*, therefore, in his judgment, not mere enemies, and he determined that the penalty should be utter destruction

But, in carrying this terrible decision into effect, he acted in a manner so deliberate, discriminating, and cautious, as to diminish very much the irritation and resentment which it would otherwise have caused, and to give it its full moral effect as a measure, not of angry resentment, but of calm and deliberate retribution—just and proper, according to the ideas of the time. In the first place, he released all the priests. Then, in respect to the rest of the population, he discriminated carefully between those who had favored the rebellion and those who had been true to their allegiance to him. The latter were allowed to depart in safety. And if, in the case of any family, it could be shown that one individual had been on the Macedonian side, the single instance of fidelity outweighed the treason of the other members, and the whole family was saved.

And the officers appointed to carry out these provisions were liberal in the interpretation and application of them, so as to save as many as there could be any possible pretext for saving. The descendants and family connections of Pindar, the celebrated poet, who has been already mentioned as having been born in Thebes, were all pardoned also, whichever side they may have taken in the contest. The truth was, that Alexander, though he had the sagacity to see that he was placed in circumstances where prodigious moral effect in strengthening his position would be produced by an act of great severity, was swayed by so many generous impulses, which raised him above the ordinary excitements of irritation and revenge, that he had every desire to make the suffering as light, and to limit it by as narrow bounds, as the nature of the case would allow. He doubtless also had an instinctive feeling that the moral effect itself of so dreadful a retribution as he was about to inflict upon the devoted city would be very much increased by forbearance and generosity, and by extreme regard for the security and protection of those who had shown themselves his friends.

After all these exceptions had been made, and the persons to whom they applied had been dismissed, the rest of the population were sold into slavery, and then the city was utterly and entirely destroyed. The number thus sold was about thirty thousand, and six thousand had been killed in the assault and storming of the city. Thus Thebes was made a ruin and a desolation, and it remained so, a monument of Alexander's terrible energy and decision, for twenty years.

The effect of the destruction of Thebes upon the other cities and states of Greece was what might have been expected. It came upon them like a thunder-bolt. Although Thebes was the only city which had openly revolted, there had been strong symptoms of disaffection in many other places. Demosthenes, who had been silent while Alexander was present in Greece, during his first visit there, had again been endeavoring to arouse opposition to Macedonian ascendency, and to concentrate and bring out into action the influences which were hostile to Alexander. He said in his speeches that Alexander was a mere boy, and that it was disgraceful for such cities as Athens, Sparta, and Thebes to submit to his sway. Alexander had heard of these things, and, as he was coming down into Greece, through the Straits of Thermopylæ, before the destruction of Thebes, he said, "They say I am a boy. I am coming to teach them that I am a man."

He did teach them that he was a man. His unexpected appearance, when they imagined him entangled among the mountains and wilds of unknown regions in the north; his sudden investiture of Thebes; the assault; the calm deliberations in respect to the destiny of the city, and the slow, cautious, discriminating, but inexorable energy with which the decision was carried into effect, all coming in such rapid succession, impressed the Grecian commonwealth with the conviction that the personage they had to deal with was no boy in character, whatever might be his years. All symptoms of disaffection against the rule of Alexander instantly disappeared, and did not soon revive again.

Nor was this effect due entirely to the terror inspired by the retribution which had been visited upon Thebes. All Greece was impressed with a new admiration for Alexander's character as they witnessed these events, in which his impetuous energy, his cool and calm decision, his forbearance, his magnanimity, and his faithfulness to his friends, were all so conspicuous. His pardoning the priests, whether they had been for him or against him, made every friend of religion incline to his favor. The same interposition in behalf of the poet's family and descendants spoke directly to the heart of every poet, orator, historian, and philosopher throughout the country, and tended to make all the lovers of literature his friends. His magnanimity, also, in deciding that one single friend of his in a family should save that family, instead of ordaining, as a more short-sighted conqueror would have done, that a single enemy should condemn it, must have awakened a strong feeling of gratitude and regard in the hearts of all who could appreciate fidelity to friends and generosity of spirit. Thus, as the news of the destruction of Thebes, and the selling of so large a portion of the inhabitants into slavery, spread over the land, its effect was to turn over so great a part of the population to a feeling of admiration of Alexander's character, and confidence in his extraordinary powers, as to leave only a small minority disposed to take sides with the punished rebels, or resent the destruction of the city.

From Thebes Alexander proceeded to the southward. Deputations from the cities were sent to him, congratulating him on his victories, and offering their adhesion to his cause. His influence and ascendency seemed firmly established now in the country of the Greeks, and in due time he returned to Macedon, and celebrated at Ægæ, which was at this time his capital, the establishment and confirmation of his power, by games, shows, spectacles, illuminations, and sacrifices to the gods, offered on a scale of the greatest pomp and magnificence. He was now ready to turn his thoughts toward the long-projected plan of the expedition into Asia.

CROSSING THE HELLESPONT

ON Alexander's arrival in Macedon, he immediately began to turn his attention to the subject of the invasion of Asia. He was full of ardor and enthusiasm to carry this project into effect. Considering his extreme youth, and the captivating character of the enterprise, it is strange that he should have exercised so much deliberation and caution as his conduct did really evince. He had now settled every thing in the most thorough manner, both within his dominions and among the nations on his borders, and, as it seemed to him, the time had come when he was to commence active preparations for the great Asiatic campaign.

He brought the subject before his ministers and counselors. They, in general, concurred with him in opinion. There were, however, two who were in doubt, or rather who were, in fact, opposed to the plan, though they expressed their non-concurrence in the form of doubts. These two persons were Antipater and Parmenio, the venerable officers who have been already mentioned as having served Philip so faithfully, and as transferring, on the death of the father, their attachment and allegiance at once to the son.

Antipater and Parmenio represented to Alexander that if he were to go to Asia at that time, he would put to extreme hazard all the interests of Macedon. As he had no family, there was, of course, no direct heir to the crown, and, in case of any misfortune happening by which his life should be lost, Macedon would become at once the prey of contending factions, which would immediately arise, each presenting its own candidate for the vacant throne. The sagacity and foresight which these statesmen evinced in these suggestions were abundantly confirmed in the end. Alexander did die in Asia, his vast kingdom at once fell into pieces, and it was desolated with internal commotions and civil wars for a long period after his death.

Parmenio and Antipater accordingly advised the king to postpone his expedition. They advised him to seek a wife among the princesses of Greece, and then to settle down quietly to the duties of domestic life, and to the government of his kingdom for a few years; then, when every thing should have become settled and consolidated in Greece, and his family was established in the hearts of his countrymen, he could leave Macedon more safely. Public affairs would go on more steadily while he lived, and, in case of his death, the crown would descend, with comparatively little danger of civil commotion, to his heir.

But Alexander was fully decided against any such policy as this. He resolved to embark in the great expedition at once. He concluded to make Antipater his vicegerent in Macedon during his absence, and to take Parmenio with him into Asia. It will be remembered that Antipater was the statesman and Parmenio the general; that is, Antipater had been employed more by Philip in civil, and Parmenio in military affairs, though in those days every body who was in public life was more or less a soldier.

Alexander left an army of ten or twelve thousand men with Antipater for the protection of Macedon. He organized another army of about thirty-five thousand to go with him. This was considered a very small army for such a vast undertaking. One or two hundred years before this time, Darius, a king of Persia, had invaded Greece with an army of five hundred thousand men, and yet he had been defeated and driven back, and now Alexander was undertaking to retaliate with a great deal less than one tenth part of the force.

Of Alexander's army of thirty-five thousand, thirty thousand were foot soldiers, and about five thousand were horse. More than half the whole army was from Macedon. The remainder was from the southern states of Greece. A large body of the horse was from Thessaly, which, as will be seen on the map, was a country south of Macedon. It was, in fact, one broad expanded valley, with mountains all around. Torrents descended from these mountains, forming streams which flowed in currents more and more deep and slow as they descended into the plains, and combining at last into one central river, which flowed to the eastward, and escaped from the environage of mountains through a most celebrated dell called the Vale of Tempe. On the north of this valley is Olympus, and on the south the two twin mountains Pelion and Ossa. There was an ancient story of a war in Thessaly between the giants who were imagined to have lived there in very early days, and the gods. The giants piled Pelion upon Ossa to enable them to get up to heaven in their assault upon their celestial enemies. The fable has led to a proverb which prevails in every language in Europe, by which all extravagant and unheard-of exertions to accomplish an end is said to be a piling of Pelion upon Ossa.

Thessaly was famous for its horses and its horsemen. The slopes of the mountains furnished the best of pasturage for the rearing of the animals, and the plains below afforded broad and open fields for training and exercising the bodies of cavalry formed by means of them. The Thessalian horse were famous throughout all Greece. Bucephalus was reared in Thessaly.

Alexander, as king of Macedon, possessed extensive estates and revenues, which were his own personal property, and were independent of the revenues of the state. Before setting out on his expedition, he apportioned these among his great officers and generals, both those who were to go and those who were to remain. He evinced great generosity in this, but it was, after all, the spirit of ambition, more than that of generosity, which led him to do it. The two great impulses which animated him were the pleasure of doing great deeds, and the fame and glory of having done them. These two principles are very distinct in their nature, though often conjoined. They were paramount and supreme in Alexander's character, and every other human principle was subordinate to them. Money was to him, accordingly, only a means to enable him to accomplish these ends. His distributing his estates and revenues in the manner above described was only a judicious appropriation of the money to the promotion of the great ends he wished to attain; it was expenditure, not gift. It answered admirably the end he had in view. His friends all looked upon him as extremely generous and self-sacrificing. They asked him what he had reserved for himself. "Hope," said Alexander.

At length all things were ready, and Alexander began to celebrate the religious sacrifices, spectacles, and shows which, in those days, always preceded great undertakings of this kind. There was a great ceremony in honor of Jupiter and the nine Muses, which had long been celebrated in Macedon as a sort of annual national festival. Alexander now caused great preparations for this festival.

In the days of the Greeks, public worship and public amusement were combined in one and the same series of spectacles and ceremonies. All worship was a theatrical show, and almost all shows were forms of worship. The religious instincts of the human heart demand some sort of sympathy and aid, real or imaginary, from the invisible world, in great and solemn undertakings, and in every momentous crisis in its history. It is true that Alexander's soldiers, about to leave their homes to go to another quarter of the globe, and into scenes of danger and death from which it was very improbable that many of them would ever return, had no other celestial protection to look up to than the spirits of ancient heroes, who, they imagined, had, somehow or other, found their final home in a sort of heaven among the summits of the mountains, where they reigned, in some sense, over human affairs; but this, small as it seems to us, was a great deal to them. They felt, when sacrificing to these gods, that they were invoking their presence and sympathy. These deities having been engaged in the same enterprises themselves, and animated with the same hopes and fears, the soldiers imagined that the semi-human divinities invoked by them would take an interest in their dangers, and rejoice in their success.

The Muses, in honor of whom, as well as Jupiter, this great Macedonian festival was held, were nine singing and dancing maidens, beautiful in countenance and form, and enchantingly graceful in all their movements. They came, the ancients imagined, from Thrace, in the north, and went first to Jupiter upon Mount Olympus, who made them goddesses. Afterward they went southward, and spread over Greece, making their residence, at last, in a palace upon Mount Parnassus, which will be found upon the map just north of the Gulf of Corinth and west of Bœotia. They were worshiped all over Greece and Italy as the goddesses of music and dancing. In later times particular sciences and arts were assigned to them respectively, as history, astronomy, tragedy, &c., though there was no distinction of this kind in early days.

The festivities in honor of Jupiter and the Muses were continued in Macedon nine days, a number corresponding with that of the dancing goddesses. Alexander made very magnificent preparations for the celebration on this occasion. He had a tent made, under which, it is said, a hundred tables could be spread; and here he entertained, day after day, an enormous company of princes, potentates, and generals. He offered sacrifices to such of the gods as he supposed it would please the soldiers to imagine that they had propitiated. Connected with these sacrifices and feastings, there were athletic and military spectacles and shows—races and wrestlings—and mock contests, with blunted spears. All these things encouraged and quickened the ardor and animation of the soldiers. It aroused their ambition to distinguish themselves by their exploits, and gave them an increased and stimulated desire for honor and fame. Thus inspirited by new desires for human praise, and trusting in the sympathy and protection of powers which were all that they conceived of as divine, the army prepared to set forth from their native land, bidding it a long, and, as it proved to most of them, a final farewell.

By following the course of Alexander's expedition upon the map at the commencement of chapter iii, it will be seen that his route lay first along the northern coasts of the Ægean Sea, He was to pass from Europe into Asia by crossing the Hellespont between Sestos and Abydos. He sent a fleet of a hundred and fifty galleys, of three banks of oars each, over the Ægean Sea, to land at Sestos, and be ready to transport his army across the straits. The army, in the mean time, marched by land. They had to cross the rivers which flow into the Ægean Sea on the northern side; but as these rivers were in Macedon, and no opposition was encountered upon the banks of them, there was no serious difficulty in effecting the passage. When they reached Sestos, they found the fleet ready there, awaiting their arrival.

It is very strikingly characteristic of the mingling of poetic sentiment and enthusiasm with calm and calculating business efficiency, which shone conspicuously so often in Alexander's career, that when he arrived at Sestos, and found that the ships were there, and the army safe, and that there was no enemy to oppose his landing on the Asiatic shore, he left Parmenio to conduct the transportation of the troops across the water, while he himself went away in a single galley on an excursion of sentiment and romantic adventure. A little south of the place where his army was to cross, there lay, on the Asiatic shore, an extended plain, on which were the ruins of Troy. Now Troy was the city which was the scene of Homer's poems—those poems which had excited so much interest in the mind of Alexander in his early years; and he determined, instead of crossing the Hellespont with the main body of his army, to proceed southward in a single galley, and land, himself, on the Asiatic shore, on the very spot which the romantic imagination of his youth had dwelt upon so often and so long.

Troy was situated upon a plain. Homer describes an island off the coast, named Tenedos, and a mountain near called Mount Ida. There was also a river called the Scamander. The island, the mountain, and the river remain, preserving their original names to the present day, except that the river is now called the Mender; but, although various vestiges of ancient ruins are found scattered about the plain, no spot can be identified as the site of the city. Some scholars have maintained that there probably never was such a city; that Homer invented the whole, there being nothing real in all that he describes except the river, the mountain, and the island. His story is, however, that there was a great and powerful city there, with a kingdom attached to it, and that this city was besieged by the Greeks for ten years, at the end of which time it was taken and destroyed.

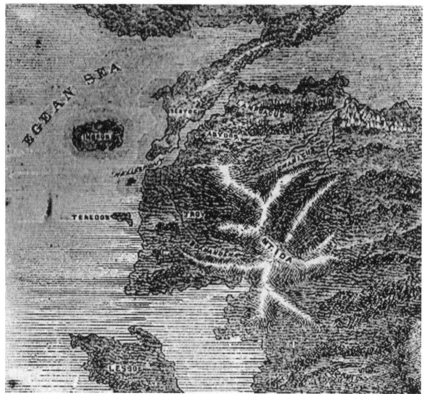

MAP OF THE PLAIN OF TROY

The story of the origin of this war is substantially this. Priam was king of Troy. His wife, a short time before her son was born, dreamed that at his birth the child turned into a torch and set the palace on fire. She told this dream to the soothsayers, and asked them what it meant. They said it must mean that her son would be the means of bringing some terrible calamities and disasters upon the family. The mother was terrified, and, to avert these calamities, gave the child to a slave as soon as it was born, and ordered him to destroy it. The slave pitied the helpless babe, and, not liking to destroy it with his own hand, carried it to Mount Ida, and left it there in the forests to die.

A she bear, roaming through the woods, found the child, and, experiencing a feeling of maternal tenderness for it, she took care of it, and reared it as if it had been her own offspring. The child was found, at last, by some shepherds who lived upon the mountain, and they adopted it as their own, robbing the brute mother of her charge. They named the boy Paris. He grew in strength and beauty, and gave early and extraordinary proofs of courage and energy, as if he had imbibed some of the qualities of his fierce foster mother with the milk she gave him. He was so remarkable for athletic beauty and manly courage, that he not only easily won the heart of a nymph of Mount Ida, named Œnone, whom he married, but he also attracted the attention of the goddesses in the heavens.

At length these goddesses had a dispute which they agreed to refer to him. The origin of the dispute was this. There was a wedding among them, and one of them, irritated at not having been invited, had a golden apple made, on which were engraved the words, "TO BE GIVEN TO THE MOST BEAUTIFUL." She threw this apple into the assembly: her object was to make them quarrel for it. In fact, she was herself the goddess of discord, and, independently of her cause of pique in this case, she loved to promote disputes. It is in allusion to this ancient tale that any subject of dispute, brought up unnecessarily among friends, is called to this day an *apple* of discord.

Three of the goddesses claimed the apple, each insisting that she was more beautiful than the others, and this was the dispute which they agreed to refer to Paris. They accordingly exhibited themselves before him in the mountains, that he might look at them and decide. They did not, however, seem willing, either of them, to trust to an impartial decision of the question, but each offered the judge a bribe to induce him to decide in her favor. One promised him a kingdom, another great fame, and the third, Venus, promised him the most beautiful woman in the world for his wife. He decided in favor of Venus; whether because she was justly entitled to the decision, or through the influence of the bribe, the story does not say.

All this time Paris remained on the mountain, a simple shepherd and herdsman, not knowing his relationship to the monarch who reigned over the city and kingdom on the plain below. King Priam, however, about this time, in some games which he was celebrating, offered, as a prize to the victor, the finest bull which could be obtained on Mount Ida. On making examination, Paris was found to have the finest bull, and the king, exercising the despotic power which kings in those days made no scruple of assuming in respect to helpless peasants, took it away. Paris was very indignant. It happened, however, that a short time afterward there was another opportunity to contend for the same bull, and Paris, disguising himself as a prince, appeared in the lists, conquered every competitor, and bore away the bull again to his home in the fastnesses of the mountain.

PARIS AND HELEN

In consequence of this his appearance at court, the daughter of Priam, whose name was Cassandra, became acquainted with him, and, inquiring into his story, succeeded in ascertaining that he was her brother, the long-lost child, that had been supposed to be put to death. King Priam was convinced by the evidence which she brought forward, and Paris was brought home to his father's house. After becombecoming established in his new position, he remembered the promise of Venus that he should have the most beautiful woman in the world for his wife, and he began, accordingly, to inquire where he could find her.

There was in Sparta, one of the cities of Southern Greece, a certain king Menelaus, who had a youthful bride named Helen, who was famed far and near for her beauty. Paris came to the conclusion that she was the most lovely woman in the world, and that he was entitled, in virtue of Venus's promise, to obtain possession of her, if he could do so by any means whatever. He accordingly made a journey into Greece, visited Sparta, formed an acquaintance with Helen, persuaded her to abandon her husband and her duty, and elope with him to Troy.

Menelaus was indignant at this outrage. He called on all Greece to take up arms and join him in the attempt to recover his bride. They responded to this demand. They first sent to Priam, demanding that he should restore Helen to her husband. Priam refused to do so, taking part with his son. The Greeks then raised a fleet and an army, and came to the plains of Troy, encamped before the city, and persevered for ten long years in besieging it, when at length it was taken and destroyed.

These stories relating to the origin of the war, however, marvelous and entertaining as they are, were not the points which chiefly interested the mind of Alexander. The portions of Homer's narratives which most excited his enthusiasm were those relating to the characters of the heroes who fought, on one side and on the other, at the siege, their various adventures, and the delineations of their motives and principles of conduct, and the emotions and excitements they experienced in the various circumstances in which they were placed. Homer described with great beauty and force the workings of ambition, of resentment, of pride, of rivalry, and all those other impulses of the human heart which would excite and control the action of impetuous men in the circumstances in which his heroes were placed.

Each one of the heroes whose history and adventures he gives, possessed a well-marked and striking character, and differed in temperament and action from the rest. Achilles was one. He was fiery, impetuous, and implacable in character, fierce and merciless; and, though perfectly undaunted and fearless, entirely destitute of magnanimity. There was a river called the Styx, the waters of which were said to have the property of making any one invulnerable. The mother of Achilles dipped him into it in his infancy, holding him by the heel. The heel, not having been immersed, was the only part which could be wounded. Thus he was safe in battle, and was a terrible warrior. He, however, quarreled with his comrades and withdrew from their cause on slight pretexts, and then became reconciled again, influenced by equally frivolous reasons.

ACHILLES

Agamemnon was the commander-in-chief of the Greek army. After a certain victory, by which some captives were taken, and were to be divided among the victors, Agamemnon was obliged to restore one, a noble lady, who had fallen to his share, and he took away the one that had been assigned to Achilles to replace her. This incensed Achilles, and he withdrew for a long time from the contest; and, in consequence of his absence, the Trojans gained great and continued victories against the Greeks. For a long time nothing could induce Achilles to return.

At length, however, though he would not go himself, he allowed his intimate friend, whose name was Patroclus, to take his armor and go into battle. Patroclus was at first successful, but was soon killed by Hector, the brother of Paris. This aroused anger and a spirit of revenge in the mind of Achilles. He gave up his quarrel with Agamemnon and returned to the combat. He did not remit his exertions till he had slain Hector, and then he expressed his brutal exultation, and satisfied his revenge, by dragging the dead body at the wheels of his chariot around the walls of the city. He then sold the body to the distracted father for a ransom.

It was such stories as these, which are related in the poems of Homer with great beauty and power, that had chiefly interested the mind of Alexander. The subjects interested him; the accounts of the contentions, the rivalries, the exploits of these warriors, the delineations of their character and springs of action, and the narrations of the various incidents and events to which such a war gave rise, were all calculated to captivate the imagination of a young martial hero.

Alexander accordingly resolved that his first landing in Asia should be at Troy. He left his army under the charge of Parmenio, to cross from Sestos to Abydos, while he himself set forth in a single galley to proceed to the southward. There was a port on the Trojan shore where the Greeks had been accustomed to disembark, and he steered his course for it. He had a bull on board his galley which he was going to offer as a sacrifice to Neptune when half way from shore to shore.

Neptune was the god of the sea. It is true that the Hellespont is not the open ocean, but it is an arm of the sea, and thus belonged properly to the dominions which the ancients assigned to the divinity of the waters. Neptune was conceived of by the ancients as a monarch dwelling on the seas or upon the coasts, and riding over the waves seated in a great shell, or sometimes in a chariot, drawn by dolphins or sea-horses. In these excursions he was attended by a train of sea-gods and nymphs, who, half floating, half swimming, followed him over the billows. Instead of a scepter Neptune carried a trident. A trident was a sort of three-pronged harpoon, such as was used in those days by the

fishermen of the Mediterranean. It was from this circumstance, probably, that it was chosen as the badge of authority for the god of the sea.

Alexander took the helm, and steered the galley with his own hands
toward the Asiatic shore. Just before he reached the land, he took his
place upon the prow, and threw a javelin at the shore as he approached
it, a symbol of the spirit of defiance and hostility with which he advanced to the frontiers of the eastern world. He was also the first to
land. After disembarking his company, he offered sacrifices to the
gods, and then proceeded to visit the places which had been the scenes
of the events which Homer had described.

Homer had written five hundred years before the time of Alexander, and there is some doubt whether the ruins and the remains of
cities which our hero found there were really the scenes of the narratives which had interested him so deeply. He, however, at any rate,
believed them to be so, and he was filled with enthusiasm and pride as
he wandered among them. He seems to have been most interested in
the character of Achilles, and he said that he envied him his happy lot
in having such a friend as Patroclus to help him perform his exploits,
and such a poet as Homer to celebrate them.

After completing his visit upon the plain of Troy, Alexander moved
toward the northeast with the few men who had accompanied him in
his single galley. In the mean time Parmenio had crossed safely, with
the main body of the army, from Sestos to Abydos. Alexander over-
took them on their march, not far from the place of their landing. To
the northward of this place, on the left of the line of march which Alexander was taking, was the city of Lampsacus.

Now a large portion of Asia Minor, although for the most part under the dominion of Persia, had been in a great measure settled by
Greeks, and, in previous wars between the two nations, the various
cities had been in possession, sometimes of one power and sometimes
of the other. In these contests the city of Lampsacus had incurred the
high displeasure of the Greeks by rebelling, as they said, on one occasion, against them. Alexander determined to destroy it as he passed.
The inhabitants were aware of this intention, and sent an embassador
to Alexander to implore his mercy. When the embassador approached,
Alexander, knowing his errand, uttered a declaration in which he
bound himself by a solemn oath not to grant the request he was about
to make. "I have come," said the embassador, "to implore you to *destroy* Lampascus." Alexander, pleased with the readiness of the
embassador in giving his language such a sudden turn, and perhaps
influenced by his oath, spared the city.

He was now fairly in Asia. The Persian forces were gathering to attack him, but so unexpected and sudden had been his invasion that they were not prepared to meet him at his arrival, and he advanced without opposition till he reached the banks of the little river Granicus.

CAMPAIGN IN ASIA MINOR

He thought it would be easiest to cross the river. It is very difficult to get a large body of horsemen and of heavy-armed soldiers, with all their attendants and baggage, over high elevations of land. This was the reason why the army turned to the northward after landing upon the Asiatic shore. Alexander thought the Granicus less of an obstacle than Mount Ida. It was not a large stream, and was easily fordable.

It was the custom in those days, as it is now when armies are marching, to send forward small bodies of men in every direction to explore the roads, remove obstacles, and discover sources of danger. These men are called, in modern times, *scouts;* in Alexander's day, and in the Greek language, they were called *prodromi,* which means fore-runners. It is the duty of these pioneers to send messengers back continually to the main body of the army, informing the officers of every thing important which comes under their observation.

In this case, when the army was gradually drawing near to the river, the *prodromi* came in with the news that they had been to the river, and found the whole opposite shore, at the place of crossing, lined with Persian troops, collected there to dispute the passage. The army continued their advance, while Alexander called the leading generals around him, to consider what was to be done.

Parmenio recommended that they should not attempt to pass the river immediately. The Persian army consisted chiefly of cavalry. Now cavalry, though very terrible as an enemy on the field of battle by day, are peculiarly exposed and defenseless in an encampment by night. The horses are scattered, feeding or at rest. The arms of the men are light, and they are not accustomed to fighting on foot; and on a sudden incursion of an enemy at midnight into their camp, their horses and their horsemanship are alike useless, and they fall an easy prey to resolute invaders. Parmenio thought, therefore, that the Persians would not dare to remain and encamp many days in the vicinity of Alexander's army, and that, accordingly, if they waited a little, the enemy would retreat, and Alexander could then cross the river without incurring the danger of a battle.

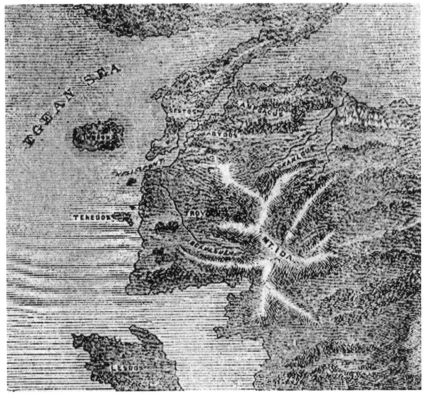

THE GRANICUS

But Alexander was unwilling to adopt any such policy. He felt confident that his army was courageous and strong enough to march on, directly through the river, ascend the bank upon the other side, and force their way through all the opposition which the Persians could make. He knew, too, that if this were done it would create a strong sensation throughout the whole country, impressing every one with a sense of the energy and power of the army which he was conducting, and would thus tend to intimidate the enemy, and facilitate all future operations. But this was not all; he had a more powerful motive still for wishing to march right on, across the river, and force his way through the vast bodies of cavalry on the opposite shore, and this was the pleasure of performing the exploit.

Accordingly, as the army advanced to the banks, they maneuvered to form in order of battle, and prepared to continue their march as if there were no obstacle to oppose them. The general order of battle of the Macedonian army was this. There was a certain body of troops, armed and organized in a peculiar manner, called the Phalanx. This body was placed in the center. The men composing it were very heavily armed. They had shields upon the left arm, and they carried spears sixteen feet long, and pointed with iron, which they held firmly in their two hands, with the points projecting far before them. The men were arranged in lines, one behind the other, and all facing the enemy— sixteen lines, and a thousand in each line, or, as it is expressed in military phrase, a thousand in rank and sixteen in file, so that the phalanx contained sixteen thousand men.

The spears were so long that when the men stood in close order, the rear ranks being brought up near to those before them, the points of the spears of eight or ten of the ranks projected in front, forming a bristling wall of points of steel, each one of which was held in its place by the strong arms of an athletic and well-trained soldier. This wall no force which could in those days be brought against it could penetrate. Men, horses, elephants, every thing that attempted to rush upon it, rushed only to their own destruction. Every spear, feeling the impulse of the vigorous arms which held it, seemed to be alive, and darted into its enemy, when an enemy was at hand, as if it felt itself the fierce hostility which directed it. If the enemy remained at a distance, and threw javelins or darts at the phalanx, they fell harmless, stopped by the shields which the soldiers wore upon the left arm, and which were held in such a manner as to form a system of scales, which covered and protected the whole mass, and made the men almost invulnerable. The phalanx was thus, when only defending itself and in a state of rest, an army and a fortification all in one, and it was almost impregnable. But when it took an aggressive form, put itself in motion, and advanced to an attack, it was infinitely more formidable. It became then a terrible monster, covered with scales of brass, from beneath which there projected forward ten thousand living, darting points of iron. It advanced deliberately and calmly, but with a prodigious momentum and force. There was nothing human in its appearance at all. It was a huge animal, ferocious, dogged, stubborn, insensible to pain, knowing no fear, and bearing down with resistless and merciless destruction upon every thing that came in its way. The phalanx was the center and soul of Al-

46

exander's army. Powerful and impregnable as it was, however, in ancient days, it would be helpless and defenseless on a modern battlefield. Solid balls of iron, flying through the air with a velocity which makes them invisible, would tear their way through the pikes and the shields, and the bodies of the men who bore them, without even feeling the obstruction.

The phalanx was subdivided into brigades, regiments, and battalions, and regularly officered. In marching, it was separated into these its constituent parts, and sometimes in battle it acted in divisions. It was stationed in the center of the army on the field, and on the two sides of it were bodies of cavalry and foot soldiers, more lightly armed than the soldiers of the phalanx, who could accordingly move with more alertness and speed, and carry their action readily wherever it might be called for. Those troops on the sides were called the wings. Alexander himself was accustomed to command one wing and Parmenio the other, while the phalanx crept along slowly but terribly between.

The army, thus arranged and organized, advanced to the river. It was a broad and shallow stream. The Persians had assembled in vast numbers on the opposite shore. Some historians say there were one hundred thousand men, others say two hundred thousand, and others six hundred thousand. However this may be there is no doubt their numbers were vastly superior to those of Alexander's army, which it will be recollected was less than forty thousand. There was a narrow plain on the opposite side of the river, next to the shore, and a range of hills beyond. The Persian cavalry covered the plain, and were ready to dash upon the Macedonian troops the moment they should emerge from the water and attempt to ascend the bank.

The army, led by Alexander, descended into the stream, and moved on through the water. They encountered the onset of their enemies on the opposite shore. A terrible and a protracted struggle ensued, but the coolness, courage, and strength of Alexander's army carried the day. The Persians were driven back, the Greeks effected their landing, reorganized and formed on the shore, and the Persians, finding that all was lost, fled in all directions.

Alexander himself took a conspicuous and a very active part in the contest. He was easily recognized on the field of battle by his dress, and by a white plume which he wore in his helmet He exposed himself to the most imminent danger. At one time, when desperately engaged with a troop of horse, which had galloped down upon him, a Persian horseman aimed a blow at his head with a sword. Alexander saved his head from the blow, but it took off his plume and a part of his helmet. Alexander immediately thrust his antagonist through the body. At the same moment, another horseman, on another side, had his sword raised, and would have killed Alexander before he could have turned to defend himself, had no help intervened; but just at this instant a third combatant, one of Alexander's friends, seeing the danger, brought down so terrible a blow upon the shoulder of this second assailant as to separate his arm from his body.

Such are the stories that are told. They may have been literally and fully true, or they may have been exaggerations of circumstances somewhat resembling them which really occurred, or they may have been fictitious altogether. Great generals, like other great men, have often the credit of many exploits which they never perform. It is the special business of poets and historians to magnify and embellish the actions of the great, and this art was understood as well in ancient days as it is now. We must remember, too, in reading the accounts of these transactions, that it is only the Greek side of the story that we hear. The Persian narratives have not come down to us.

At any rate, the Persian army was defeated, and that, too, without the assistance of the phalanx. The horsemen and the light troops were alone engaged. The phalanx could not be formed, nor could it act in such a position. The men, on emerging from the water, had to climb up the banks, and rush on to the attack of an enemy consisting of squadrons of horse ready to dash at once upon them.

The Persian army was defeated and driven away. Alexander did not pursue them. He felt that he had struck a very heavy blow. The news of this defeat of the Persians would go with the speed of the wind all over Asia Minor, and operate most powerfully in his favor. He sent home to Greece an account of the victory, and with the account he forwarded three hundred suits of armor, taken from the Persian horsemen killed on the field. These suits of armor were to be hung up in the Parthenon, a great temple at Athens; the most conspicuous position for them, perhaps, which all Europe could afford.

The name of the Persian general who commanded at the battle of the Granicus was Memnon. He had been opposed to the plan of hazarding a battle. Alexander had come to Asia with no provisions and no money. He had relied on being able to sustain his army by his victories. Memnon, therefore, strongly urged that the Persians should retreat slowly, carrying off all the valuable property, and destroying all that could not be removed, taking especial care to leave no provisions behind them. In this way he thought that the army of Alexander would be reduced by privation and want, and would, in the end, fall an easy prey. His opinion was, however, overruled by the views of the other commanders, and the battle of the Granicus was the consequence.

Alexander encamped to refresh his army and to take care of the wounded. He went to see the wounded men one by one, inquired into the circumstances of each case, and listened to each one who was able to talk, while he gave an account of his adventures in the battle, and the manner in which he received his wound. To be able thus to tell their story to their general, and to see him listening to it with interest and pleasure, filled their hearts with pride and joy; and the whole army was inspired with the highest spirit of enthusiasm, and with eager desires to have another opportunity occur in which they could encounter danger and death in the service of such a leader. It is in such traits as these that the true greatness of the soul of Alexander shines. It must be remembered that all this time he was but little more than twenty-one. He was but just of age.

From his encampment on the Granicus Alexander turned to the southward, and moved along on the eastern shores of the Ægean Sea. The country generally surrendered to him without opposition. In fact, it was hardly Persian territory at all. The inhabitants were mainly of Greek extraction, and had been sometimes under Greek and sometimes under Persian rule. The conquest of the country resulted simply in a change of the executive officer of each province. Alexander took special pains to lead the people to feel that they had nothing to fear from him. He would not allow the soldiers to do any injury. He protected all private property. He took possession only of the citadels, and of such governmental property as he found there, and he continued the same taxes, the same laws, and the same tribunals as had existed before his invasion. The cities and the provinces accordingly surrendered to him as he passed along, and in a very short time all the western part of Asia Minor submitted peacefully to his sway.

The narrative of this progress, as given by the ancient historians, is diversified by a great variety of adventures and incidents, which give great interest to the story, and strikingly illustrate the character of Alexander and the spirit of the times. In some places there would be a contest between the Greek and the Persian parties before Alexander's arrival. At Ephesus the animosity had been so great that a sort of civil war had broken out. The Greek party had gained the ascendency, and were threatening a general massacre of the Persian inhabitants. Alexander promptly interposed to protect them, though they were his enemies. The intelligence of this act of forbearance and generosity spread all over the land, and added greatly to the influence of Alexander's name, and to the estimation in which he was held.

It was the custom in those days for the mass of the common soldiers to be greatly influenced by what they called *omens*, that is, signs and tokens which they observed in the flight or the actions of birds, and other similar appearances. In one case, the fleet, which had come along the sea, accompanying the march of the army on land, was pent up in a harbor by a stronger Persian fleet outside. One of the vessels of the Macedonian fleet was aground. An eagle lighted upon the mast, and stood perched there for a long time, looking toward the sea. Parmenio said that, as the eagle looked toward the sea, it indicated that victory lay in that quarter, and he recommended that they should arm their ships and push boldly out to attack the Persians. But Alexander maintained that, as the eagle alighted on a ship which was aground, it indicated that they were to look for their success on the shore. The omens could thus almost always be interpreted any way, and sagacious generals only sought in them the means of confirming the courage and confidence of their soldiers, in respect to the plans which they adopted under the influence of other considerations altogether. Alexander knew very well that he was not a sailor, and had no desire to embark on contests from which, however they might end, he would himself personally obtain no glory.

When the winter came on, Alexander and his army were about three or four hundred miles from home; and, as he did not intend to advance much farther until the spring should open, he announced to the army that all those persons, both officers and soldiers who had been married within the year, might go home if they chose, and spend the winter with their brides, and return to the army in the spring. No doubt this was an admirable stroke of policy; for, as the number could not be large, their absence could not materially weaken his force, and they would, of course, fill all Greece with tales of Alexander's energy and courage, and of the nobleness and generosity of his character. It was the most effectual way possible of disseminating through Europe the most brilliant accounts of what he had already done.

Besides, it must have awakened a new bond of sympathy and fellow-feeling between himself and his soldiers, and greatly increased the attachment to him felt both by those who went and those who remained. And though Alexander must have been aware of all these advantages of the act, still no one could have thought of or adopted such a plan unless he was accustomed to consider and regard, in his dealings with others, the feelings and affections of the heart, and to cherish a warm sympathy for them. The bridegroom soldiers, full of exultation and pleasure, set forth on their return to Greece, in a detachment under the charge of three generals, themselves bridegrooms too.

Alexander, however, had no idea of remaining idle during the winter. He marched on from province to province, and from city to city, meeting with every variety of adventures. He went first along the southern coast, until at length he came to a place where a mountain chain, called Taurus, comes down to the sea-coast, where it terminates abruptly in cliffs and precipices, leaving only a narrow beach between them and the water below. This beach was sometimes covered and sometimes bare. It is true, there is very little tide in the Mediterranean, but the level of the water along the shores is altered considerably by the long-continued pressure exerted in one direction or another by winds and storms. The water was *up* when Alexander reached this pass; still he determined to march his army through it. There was another way, back among the mountains, but Alexander seemed disposed to gratify the love of adventure which his army felt, by introducing them to a novel scene of danger. They accordingly defiled along under these cliffs, marching, as they say, sometimes up to the waist in water, the swell rolling in upon them all the time from the offing.

Having at length succeeded in passing safely round this frowning buttress of the mountains, Alexander turned northward, and advanced into the very heart of Asia Minor. In doing this he had to pass *over* the range which he had come *round* before; and, as it was winter, his army were, for a time, enveloped in snows and storms among the wild and frightful defiles. They had here, in addition to the dangers and hardships of the way and of the season, to encounter the hostility of their foes, as the tribes who inhabited these mountains assembled to dispute the passage. Alexander was victorious, and reached a valley through which there flows a river which has handed down its name to the English language and literature. This river was the Meander. Its beautiful windings through verdant and fertile valleys were so renowned, that every stream which imitates its example is said to *meander* to the present day.

During all this time Parmenio had remained in the western part of Asia Minor with a considerable body of the army. As the spring approached, Alexander sent him orders to go to Gordium, whither he was himself proceeding, and meet him there. He also directed that the detachment which had gone home should, on recrossing the Hellespont on their return, proceed eastward to Gordium, thus making that city the general rendezvous for the commencement of his next campaign.

One reason why Alexander desired to go to Gordium was that he wished to untie the famous Gordian knot. The story of the Gordian knot was this. Gordius was a sort of mountain farmer. One day he was plowing, and an eagle came down and alighted upon his yoke, and remained there until he had finished his plowing This was an omen, but what was the signification of it? Gordius did not know, and he accordingly went to a neighboring town in order to consult the prophets and soothsayers. On his way he met a damsel, who, like Rebecca in the days of Abraham, was going forth to draw water. Gordius fell into conversation with her, and related to her the occurrence which had interested him so strongly. The maiden advised him to go back and offer a sacrifice to Jupiter. Finally, she consented to go back with him and aid him. The affair ended in her becoming his wife, and they lived together in peace for many years upon their farm.

They had a son named Midas. The father and mother were accustomed to go out sometimes in their cart or wagon, drawn by the oxen, Midas driving. One day they were going into the town in this way, at a time when it happened that there was an assembly convened, which was in a state of great perplexity on account of the civil dissensions and contests which prevailed in the country. They had just inquired of an oracle what they should do. The oracle said that "a cart would bring them a king, who would terminate their eternal broils." Just then Midas came up, driving the cart in which his father and mother were seated. The assembly thought at once that this must be the cart meant by the oracle, and they made Gordius king by acclamation. They took the cart and the yoke to preserve as sacred relics, consecrating them to Jupiter; and Gordius tied the yoke to the pole of the cart by a thong of leather, making a knot so close and complicated that nobody could untie it again. It was called the Gordian knot. The oracle afterward said that whoever should untie this knot should become monarch of all Asia. Thus far, nobody had succeeded.

Alexander felt a great desire to see this knot and try what he could do. He went, accordingly, into the temple where the sacred cart had been deposited, and, after looking at the knot, and satisfying himself that the task of untying it was hopeless, he cut it to pieces with his sword. How far the circumstances of this whole story are true, and how far fictitious, no one can tell; the story itself, however, as thus related, has come down from generation to generation, in every country of Europe, for two thousand years, and any extrication of one's self from a difficulty by violent means has been called cutting the Gordian knot to the present day.

At length the whole army was assembled, and the king recommenced his progress. He went on successfully for some weeks, moving in a southeasterly direction, and bringing the whole country under his dominion, until, at length, when he reached Tarsus, an event occurred which nearly terminated his career. There were some circumstances which caused him to press forward with the utmost effort in approaching Tarsus, and, as the day was warm, he got very much overcome with heat and fatigue. In this state, he went and plunged suddenly into the River Cydnus to bathe.

THE BATHING IN THE RIVER CYDNUS

Now the Cydnus is a small stream, flowing by Tarsus, and it comes down from Mount Taurus at a short distance back from the city. Such streams are always very cold. Alexander was immediately seized with a very violent chill, and was taken out of the water shivering excessively, and, at length, fainted away. They thought he was dying. They bore him to his tent, and, as tidings of their leader's danger spread through the camp, the whole army, officers and soldiers, were thrown into the greatest consternation and grief.

A violent and protracted fever came on. In the course of it, an incident occurred which strikingly illustrates the boldness and originality of Alexander's character. The name of his physician was Philip. Philip had been preparing a particular medicine for him, which, it seems, required some days to make ready. Just before it was presented, Alexander received a letter from Parmenio, informing him that he had good reason to believe that Philip had been bribed by the Persians to murder him, during his sickness, by administering poison in the name of medicine. He wrote, he said, to put him on his guard against any medicine which Philip might offer him.

Alexander put the letter under his pillow, and communicated its contents to no one. At length, when the medicine was ready, Philip brought it in. Alexander took the cup containing it with one hand, and with the other he handed Philip the communication which he had received from Parmenio, saying, "Read that letter." As soon as Philip had finished reading it, and was ready to look up, Alexander drank off the draught in full, and laid down the cup with an air of perfect confidence that he had nothing to fear.

Some persons think that Alexander watched the countenance of his physician while he was reading the letter, and that he was led to take the medicine by his confidence in his power to determine the guilt or the innocence of a person thus accused by his looks. Others suppose that the act was an expression of his implicit faith in the integrity and fidelity of his servant, and that he intended it as testimony, given in a very pointed and decisive, and, at the same time, delicate manner, that he was not suspicious of his friends, or easily led to distrust their faithfulness. Philip was, at any rate, extremely gratified at the procedure, and Alexander recovered.

Alexander had now traversed the whole extent of Asia Minor, and had subdued the entire country to his sway. He was now advancing to another district, that of Syria and Palestine, which lies on the eastern shores of the Mediteranean Sea. To enter this new territory, he had to pass over a narrow plain which lay between the mountains and the sea, at a place called Issus. Here he was met by the main body of the Persian army, and the great battle of Issus was fought. This battle will be the subject of the next chapter.

DEFEAT OF DARIUS

THUS far Alexander had had only the lieutenants and generals of the Persian monarch to contend with. Darius had at first looked upon the invasion of his vast dominions by such a mere boy, as he called him, and by so small an army, with contempt. He sent word to his generals in Asia Minor to seize the young fool, and send him to Persia bound hand and foot. By the time, however, that Alexander had possessed himself of all Asia Minor, Darius began to find that, though young, he was no fool, and that it was not likely to be very easy to seize him.

Accordingly, Darius collected an immense army himself, and advanced to meet the Macedonians in person. Nothing could exceed the pomp and magnificence of his preparations. There were immense numbers of troops, and they were of all nations. There were even a great many Greeks among his forces, many of them enlisted from the Greeks of Asia Minor. There were some from Greece itself— mercenaries, as they were called; that is, soldiers who fought for pay, and who were willing to enter into any service which would pay them best.

There were even some Greek officers and counselors in the family and court of Darius. One of them, named Charidemus, offended the king very much by the free opinion which he expressed of the uselessness of all his pomp and parade in preparing for an encounter with such an enemy as Alexander. "Perhaps," said Charidemus, "you may not be pleased with my speaking to you plainly, but if I do not do it now, it will be too late hereafter. This great parade and pomp, and this enormous multitude of men, might be formidable to your Asiatic neighbors; but such sort of preparation will be of little avail against Alexander and his Greeks. Your army is resplendent with purple and gold. No one who had not seen it could conceive of its magnificence; but it will not be of any avail against the terrible energy of the Greeks.

Their minds are bent on something very different from idle show. They are intent on securing the substantial excellence of their weapons, and on acquiring the discipline and the hardihood essential for the most efficient use of them. They will despise all your parade of purple and gold. They will not even value it as plunder. They glory in their ability to dispense with all the luxuries and conveniences of life. They live upon the coarsest food. At night they sleep upon the bare ground. By day they are always on the march. They brave hunger, cold, and every species of exposure with pride and pleasure, having the greatest contempt for any thing like softness and effeminacy of character. All this pomp and pageantry, with inefficient weapons, and inefficient men to wield them, will be of no avail against their invincible courage and energy; and the best disposition that you can make of all your gold, and silver, and other treasures, is to send it away and procure good soldiers with it, if indeed gold and silver will procure them."

The Greeks were habituated to energetic speaking as well as acting, but Charidemus did not sufficiently consider that the Persians were not accustomed to hear such plain language as this. Darius was very much displeased. In his anger he condemned him to death. "Very well," said Charidemus, "I can die. But my avenger is at hand. My advice is good, and Alexander will soon punish you for not regarding it."

Very gorgeous descriptions are given of the pomp and magnificence of the army of Darius, as he commenced his march from the Euphrates to the Mediterranean. The Persians worship the sun and fire. Over the king's tent there was an image of the sun in crystal, and supported in such a manner as to be in the view of the whole army. They had also silver altars, on which they kept constantly burning what they called the sacred fire. These altars were borne by persons appointed for the purpose, who were clothed in magnificent costumes. Then came a long procession of priests and magi, who were dressed also in very splendid robes. They performed the services of public worship. Following them came a chariot consecrated to the sun. It was drawn by white horses, and was followed by a single white horse of large size and noble form, which was a sacred animal, being called the horse of the sun. The equerries, that is, the attendants who had charge of this horse, were also all dressed in white, and each carried a golden rod in his hand.

There were bodies of troops distinguished from the rest, and occupying positions of high honor, but these were selected and advanced above the others, not on account of their courage, or strength, or superior martial efficiency, but from considerations connected with their birth, and rank, and other aristocratic qualities. There was one body called the Kinsmen, who were the relatives of the king, or, at least, so considered, though, as there were fifteen thousand of them, it would seem that the relationship could not have been, in all cases, very near. They were dressed with great magnificence, and prided themselves on their rank, their wealth, and the splendor of their armor. There was also a corps called the Immortals. They were ten thousand in number. They wore a dress of gold tissue, which glittered with spangles and precious stones.

These bodies of men, thus dressed, made an appearance more like that of a civic procession, on an occasion of ceremony and rejoicing, than like the march of an army. The appearance of the king in his chariot was still more like an exhibition of pomp and parade. The carriage was very large, elaborately carved and gilded, and ornamented with statues and sculptures. Here the king sat on a very elevated seat, in sight of all. He was clothed in a vest of purple, striped with silver, and over his vest he wore a robe glittering with gold and precious stones. Around his waist was a golden girdle, from which was suspended his cimeter—a species of sword—the scabbard of which was resplendent with gems. He wore a tiara upon his head of very costly and elegant workmanship, and enriched, like the rest of his dress, with brilliant ornaments. The guards who preceded and followed him had pikes of silver, mounted and tipped with gold.

It is very extraordinary that King Darius took his wife and all his family with him, and a large portion of his treasures, on this expedition against Alexander. His mother, whose name was Sysigambis, was in his family, and she and his wife came, each in her own chariot, immediately after the king. Then there were fifteen carriages filled with the children and their attendants, and three or four hundred ladies of the court, all dressed like queens. After the family there came a train of many hundreds of camels and mules, carrying the royal treasures.

It was in this style that Darius set out upon his expedition, and he advanced by a slow progress toward the westward, until at length he approached the shores of the Mediterranean Sea. He left his treasures in the city of Damascus, where they were deposited under the charge of a sufficient force to protect them, as he supposed. He then advanced to meet Alexander, going himself from Syria toward Asia Minor just at the time that Alexander was coming from Asia Minor into Syria.

It will be observed by looking upon the map that the chain of mountains called Mount Taurus extends down near to the coast, at the northeastern corner of the Mediterranean. Among these mountains there are various tracts of open country, through which an army may march to and fro, between Syria and Asia Minor. Now it happened that

PLAIN OF ISSUS

Darius, in going toward the west, took a more inland route than Alexander, who, on coming eastward, kept nearer to the sea. Alexander did not know that Darius was so near; and as for Darius, he was confident that Alexander was retreating before him; for, as the Macedonian army was so small, and his own forces constituted such an innumerable host, the idea that Alexander would remain to brave a battle was, in his opinion, entirely out of the question. He had, therefore, no doubt that Alexander was retreating. It is, of course, always difficult for two armies, fifty miles apart, to obtain correct ideas of each other's movements. All the ordinary intercommunications of the country are of course stopped, and each general has his scouts out, with orders to intercept all travelers, and to interrupt the communication of intelligence by every means in their power.

In consequence of these and other circumstances of a similar nature, it happened that Alexander and Darius actually passed each other, without either of them being aware of it. Alexander advanced into Syria by the plains of Issus, marked *a* upon the map, and a narrow pass beyond, called the Gates of Syria, while Darius went farther to the north, and arrived at Issus after Alexander had left it. Here each army learned to their astonishment that their enemy was in their rear. Alexander could not credit this report when he first heard it. He dispatched a galley with thirty oars along the shore, up the Gulf of Issus, to ascertain the truth. The galley soon came back and reported that, beyond the Gates of Syria, they saw the whole country, which was nearly level land, though gently rising from the sea, covered with the vast encampments of the Persian army.

The king then called his generals and counselors together, informed them of the facts, and made known to them his determination to return immediately through the Gates of Syria and attack the Persian army. The officers received the intelligence with enthusiastic expressions of joy.

It was now near the evening. Alexander sent forward a strong reconnoitering party, ordering them to proceed cautiously, to ascend eminences and look far before them, to guard carefully against surprise, and to send back word immediately if they came upon any traces of the enemy. At the present day the operations of such a reconnoitering party are very much aided by the use of spy-glasses, which are made now with great care expressly for military purposes. The instrument, however, was not known in Alexander's day.

When the evening came on, Alexander followed the reconnoitering party with the main body of the army. At midnight they reached the defile. When they were secure in the possession of it, they halted. Strong watches were stationed on all the surrounding heights to guard against any possible surprise. Alexander himself ascended one of the eminences, from whence he could look down upon the great plain beyond, which was dimly illuminated in every part by the smouldering fires of the Persian encampment. An encampment at night is a spectacle which is always grand, and often sublime. It must have appeared sublime to Alexander in the highest degree, on this occasion. To stand stealthily among these dark and somber mountains, with the defiles and passes below filled with the columns of his small but undaunted army, and to look onward, a few miles beyond, and see the countless fires of the vast hosts which had got between him and all hope of retreat to his native land; to feel, as he must have done, that his fate, and that of all who were with him, depended upon the events of the day that was soon to dawn—to see and feel these things must have made this night one of the most exciting and solemn scenes in the conqueror's life. He had a soul to enjoy its excitement and sublimity. He gloried in it; and, as if he wished to add to the solemnity of the scene, he caused an altar to be erected, and offered a sacrifice, by torch-light, to the deities on whose aid his soldiers imagined themselves most dependent for success on the morrow. Of course a place was selected where the lights of the torches would not attract the attention of the enemy, and sentinels were stationed at every advantageous point to watch the Persian camp for the slightest indications of movement or alarm.

In the morning, at break of day, Alexander commenced his march down to the plain. In the evening, at sunset, all the valleys and defiles among the mountains around the plain of Issus were thronged with vast masses of the Persian army, broken, disordered, and in confusion, all pressing forward to escape from the victorious Macedonians. They crowded all the roads, they choked up the mountain passes, they trampled upon one another, they fell, exhausted with fatigue and mental agitation. Darius was among them, though his flight had been so sudden that he had left his mother, and his wife, and all his family behind. He pressed on in his chariot as far as the road allowed his chariot to go, and then, leaving every thing behind, he mounted a horse and rode on for his life.

Alexander and his army soon abandoned the pursuit, and returned to take possession of the Persian camp. The tents of King Darius and his household were inconceivably splendid, and were filled with gold and silver vessels, caskets, vases, boxes of perfumes, and every imaginable article of luxury and show. The mother and wife of Darius bewailed their hard fate with cries and tears, and continued all the evening in an agony of consternation and despair.

Alexander, hearing of this, sent Leonnatus, his former teacher, a man of years and gravity, to quiet their fears and comfort them, so far as it was possible to comfort them. In addition to their own captivity, they supposed that Darius was killed, and the mother was mourning bitterly for her son, and the wife for her husband. Leonnatus, attended by some soldiers, advanced toward the tent where these mourners were dwelling. The attendants at the door ran in and informed them that a body of Greeks were coming. This threw them into the greatest consternation. They anticipated violence and death, and threw themselves upon the ground in agony. Leonnatus waited some time at the door for the attendants to return. At length he entered the tent. This renewed the terrors of the women. They began to entreat him to spare their lives, at least until there should be time for them to see the remains of the son and husband whom they mourned, and to pay the last sad tribute to his memory.

Leonnatus soon relieved their fears. He told them that he was charged by Alexander to say to them that Darius was alive, having made his escape in safety. As to themselves, Alexander assured them, he said, that they should not be injured; that not only were their persons and lives to be protected, but no change was to he made in their condition or mode of life; they should continue to be treated like queens. He added, moreover, that Alexander wished him to say that he felt no animosity or ill will whatever against Darius. He was but technically his enemy, being only engaged in a generous and honorable contest with him for the empire of Asia. Saying these things, Leonnatus raised the disconsolate ladies from the ground, and they gradually regained some degree of composure.

Alexander himself went to pay a visit to the captive princesses the next day. He took with him Hephæstion. Hephæstion was Alexander's personal friend. The two young men were of the same age, and, though Alexander had the good sense to retain in power all the old and experienced officers which his father had employed, both in the court and army, he showed that, after all, ambition had not overwhelmed and stifled all the kindlier feelings of the heart, by his strong attachment to this young companion. Hephæstion was his confidant, his associate, his personal friend. He did what very few monarchs have done, either before or since, in securing for himself the pleasures of friendship, and of intimate social communion with a heart kindred to his own, without ruining himself by committing to a favorite powers which he was not qualified to wield. Alexander left the wise and experienced Parmenio to manage the camp, while he took the young and handsome Hephæstion to accompany him on his visit to the captive queens.

When the two friends entered the tent, the ladies were, from some cause, deceived, and mistook Hephæstion for Alexander, and addressed him, accordingly, with tokens of high respect and homage. One of their attendants immediately rectified the mistake, telling them that the other was Alexander. The ladies were at first overwhelmed with confusion, and attempted to apologize; but the king reassured them at once by the easy and good-natured manner with which he passed over the mistake, saying it was no mistake at all. "It is true," said he, "that I am Alexander, but then he is Alexander too."

The wife of Darius was young and very beautiful, and they had a little son who was with them in the camp. It seems almost unaccountable that Darius should have brought such a helpless and defenseless charge with him into camps and fields of battle. But the truth was that he had no idea of even a battle with Alexander, and as to defeat, he did not contemplate the remotest possibility of it. He regarded Alexander as a mere boy—energetic and daring it is true, and at the head of a desperate band of adventurers; but he considered his whole force as altogether too insignificant to make any stand against such a vast military power as he was bringing against him. He presumed that he would retreat, as fast as possible before the Persian army came near him. The idea of such a boy coming down at break of day, from narrow defiles of the mountains, upon his vast encampment covering all the plains, and in twelve hours putting the whole mighty mass to flight, was what never entered his imagination at all. The exploit was, indeed, a very extraordinary one. Alexander's forces may have consisted of forty or fifty thousand men, and, if we may believe their story, there were over a hundred thousand Persians left dead upon the field. Many of these were, however, killed by the dreadful confusion and violence of the retreat, as vast bodies of horsemen, pressing through the defiles, rode over and trampled down the foot soldiers who were toiling in awful confusion along the way, having fled before the horsemen left the field.

Alexander had heard that Darius had left the greater part of his royal treasures in Damascus, and he sent Parmenio there to seize them. This expedition was successful. An enormous amount of gold and silver fell into Alexander's hands. The plate was coined into money, and many of the treasures were sent to Greece.

Darius got together a small remnant of his army and continued his flight. He did not stop until he had crossed the Euphrates. He then sent an embassador to Alexander to make propositions for peace. He remonstrated with him, in the communication which he made, for coming thus to invade his dominions, and urged him to withdraw and be satisfied with his own kingdom. He offered him any sum he might name as a ransom for his mother, wife, and child, and agreed that if he would deliver them up to him on the payment of the ransom, and depart from his dominions, he would thenceforth regard him as an ally and a friend.

Alexander replied by a letter, expressed in brief but very decided language. He said that the Persians had, under the ancestors of Darius crossed the Hellespont, invaded Greece, laid waste the country, and destroyed cities and towns, and had thus done them incalculable injury; and that Darius himself had been plotting against his (Alexander's) life, and offering rewards to any one who would kill him. "I am acting, then," continued Alexander, "only on the defensive. The gods, who always favor the right, have given me the victory. I am now monarch of a large part of Asia, and your sovereign king. If you will admit this, and come to me as my subject, I will restore to you your mother, your wife, and your child, without any ransom. And, at any rate, whatever you decide in respect to these proposals, if you wish to communicate with me on any subject hereafter, I shall pay no attention to what you send unless you address it to me as your king."

One circumstance occurred at the close of this great victory which illustrates the magnanimity of Alexander's character, and helps to explain the very strong personal attachment which every body within the circle of his influence so obviously felt for him. He found a great number of envoys and embassadors from the various states of Greece at the Persian court, and these persons fell into his hands among the other captives. Now the states and cities of Greece, all except Sparta and Thebes, which last city he had destroyed, were combined ostensibly in the confederation by which Alexander was sustained. It seems, however, that there was a secret enmity against him in Greece, and various parties had sent messengers and agents to the Persian court to aid in plots and schemes to interfere with and defeat Alexander's plans. The Thebans, scattered and disorganized as they were, had sent envoys in this way. Now Alexander, in considering what disposition he should make of these emissaries from his own land, decided to regard them all as traitors except the Thebans. All except the Thebans were *traitors*, he maintained, for acting secretly against him, while ostensibly, and by solemn covenants, they were his friends. "The case of the Thebans is very different," said he. "I have destroyed their city, and they have a right to consider me their enemy, and to do all they can to oppose my progress, and to regain their own lost existence and their former power." So he gave them their liberty and sent them away with marks of consideration and honor.

As the vast army of the Persian monarch had now been defeated, of course none of the smaller kingdoms or provinces thought of resisting.

They yielded one after another, and Alexander appointed governors of his own to rule over them. He advanced in this manner along the eastern shores of the Mediterranean Sea, meeting with no obstruction until he reached the great and powerful city of Tyre.

THE SIEGE OF TYRE

Tyre had been built originally on the mainland; but in some of the wars which it had to encounter with the kings of Babylon in the East, this old city had been abandoned by the inhabitants, and a new one built upon an island not far from the shore, which could be more easily defended from an enemy. The old city had gone to ruin, and its place was occupied by old walls, fallen towers, stones, columns, arches, and other remains of the ancient magnificence of the place.

The island on which the Tyre of Alexander's day had been built was about half a mile from the shore. The water between was about eighteen feet deep, and formed a harbor for the vessels. The great business of the Tyrians was commerce. They bought and sold merchandise in all the ports of the Mediterranean Sea, and transported it by their merchant vessels to and fro. They had also fleets of war galleys, which they used to protect their interests on the high seas, and in the various ports which their merchant vessels visited. They were thus wealthy and powerful, and yet they lived shut up upon their little island, and were almost entirely independent of the main-land.

The city itself, however, though contracted in extent on account of the small dimensions of the island, was very compactly built and strongly fortified, and it contained a vast number of stately and magnificent edifices, which were filled with stores of wealth that had been accumulated by the mercantile enterprise and thrift of many generations. Extravagant stories are told by the historians and geographers of those days, in respect to the scale on which the structures of Tyre were built. It was said, for instance, that the walls were one hundred and fifty feet high. It is true that the walls rose directly from the surface of the water, and of course a considerable part of their elevation was required to bring them up to the level of the surface of the land; and then, in addition to this, they had to be carried up the whole ordinary height of a city wall to afford the usual protection to the edifices and dwellings within. There might have been some places where the walls themselves, or structures connected with them, were carried up to the elevation above named, though it is scarcely to be supposed that such could have been their ordinary dimensions.

At any rate, Tyre was a very wealthy, magnificent, and powerful city, intent on its commercial operations, and well furnished with means of protecting them at sea, but feeling little interest, and taking little part, in the contentions continually arising among the rival powers which had possession of the land. Their policy was to retain their independence, and yet to keep on good terms with all other powers, so that their commercial intercourse with the ports of all nations might go on undisturbed.

It was, of course, a very serious question with Alexander, as his route lay now through Phœnicia and in the neighborhood of Tyre, what he should do in respect to such a port. He did not like to leave it behind him and proceed to the eastward; for, in case of any reverses happening to him, the Tyrians would be very likely to act decidedly against him, and their power on the Mediterranean would enable them to act very efficiently against him on all the coasts of Greece and Asia Minor. On the other hand, it seemed a desperate undertaking to attack the city. He had none but land forces, and the island was half a mile from the shore. Besides, its enormous walls, rising perpendicularly out of the water, it was defended by ships well armed and manned. It was not possible to surround the city and starve it into submission, as the inhabitants had wealth to buy, and ships to bring in, any quantity of provisions and stores by sea. Alexander, however, determined not to follow Darius toward the east, and leave such a stronghold as this behind him.

The Tyrians wished to avoid a quarrel if it were possible. They sent complimentary messages to Alexander, congratulating him on his conquests, and disavowing all feelings of hostility to him. They also sent him a golden crown, as many of the other states of Asia had done, in token of their yielding a general submission to his authority. Alexander returned very gracious replies, and expressed to them his intention of coming to Tyre for the purpose of offering sacrifices, as he said, to Hercules, a god whom the Tyrians worshiped.

The Tyrians knew that wherever Alexander went he went at the head of his army, and his coming into Tyre at all implied necessarily his taking military possession of it. They thought it might, perhaps, be somewhat difficult to dispossess such a visitor after he should once get installed in their castles and palaces. So they sent him word that it would not be in their power to receive him in the city itself, but that he could offer the sacrifice which he intended on the main-land, as there was a temple sacred to Hercules among the ruins there.

Alexander then called a council of his officers, and stated to them his views. He said that, on reflecting fully upon the subject, he had come to the conclusion that it was best to postpone pushing his expedition forward into the heart of Persia until he should have subdued Tyre completely, and made himself master of the Mediterranean Sea. He said, also, that he should take possession of Egypt before turning his arms toward the forces that Darius was gathering against him in the East. The generals of the army concurred in this opinion, and Alexander advanced toward Tyre. The Tyrians prepared for their defense.

After examining carefully all the circumstances of the case, Alexander conceived the very bold plan of building a broad causeway from the main-land to the island on which the city was founded, out of the ruins of old Tyre, and then marching his army over upon it to the walls of the city, where he could then plant his engines and make a breach. This would seem to be a very desperate undertaking. It is true the stones remaining on the site of the old city afforded sufficient materials for the construction of the pier, but then the work must go on against a tremendous opposition, both from the walls of the city itself and from the Tyrian ships in the harbor. It would seem to be almost impossible to protect the men from these attacks so as to allow the operations to proceed at all, and the difficulty and danger must increase very rapidly as the work should approach the walls of the city. But, notwithstanding these objections, Alexander determined to proceed. Tyre must be taken, and this was obviously the only possible mode of taking it.

The soldiers advanced to undertake the work with great readiness. Their strong personal attachment to Alexander; their confidence that whatever he should plan and attempt would succeed; the novelty and boldness of this design of reaching an island by building an isthmus to it from the main-land—these and other similar considerations excited the ardor and enthusiasm of the troops to the highest degree.

In constructing works of this kind in the water, the material used is sometimes stone and sometimes earth. So far as earth is employed, it is necessary to resort to some means to prevent its spreading under the water, or being washed away by the dash of the waves at its sides. This is usually effected by driving what are called *piles*, which are long beams of wood, pointed at the end, and driven into the earth by means of powerful engines. Alexander sent parties of men into the mountains of Lebanon, where were vast forests of cedars, which were very celebrated in ancient times, and which are often alluded to in the sacred scriptures. They cut down these trees, and brought the stems of them to the shore, where they sharpened them at one end and drove them into the sand, in order to protect the sides of their embankment. Others brought stones from the ruins and tumbled them into the sea in the direction where the pier was to be built. It was some time before the work made such progress as to attract much attention from Tyre. At length, however, when the people of the city saw it gradually increasing in size and advancing toward them, they concluded that they must engage in earnest in the work of arresting its progress.

They accordingly constructed engines on the walls to throw heavy darts and stones over the water to the men upon the pier. They sent secretly to the tribes that inhabited the valleys and ravines among the mountains, to attack the parties at work there, and they landed forces from the city at some distance from the pier, and then marched along the shore, and attempted to drive away the men that were engaged in carrying stones from the ruins. They also fitted up and manned some galleys of large size, and brought them up near to the pier itself, and attacked the men who were at work upon it with stones, darts, arrows, and missiles of every description.

But all was of no avail. The work, though impeded, still went on. Alexander built large screens of wood upon the pier, covering them with hides, which protected his soldiers from the weapons of the enemy, so that they could carry on their operations safely behind them. By these means the work advanced for some distance further. As it advanced, various structures were erected upon it, especially along the sides and at the end toward the city. These structures consisted of great engines for driving piles, and machines for throwing stones and darts, and towers carried up to a great height, to enable the men to throw stones and heavy weapons down upon the galleys which might attempt to approach them.

At length the Tyrians determined on attempting to destroy all these wooden works by means of what is called in modern times a *fire ship*. They took a large galley, and filled it with combustibles of every kind. They loaded it first with light dry wood, and they poured pitch, and tar, and oil over all this wood to make it burn with fiercer flames. They saturated the sails and the cordage in the same manner, and laid trains of combustible materials through all parts of the vessel, so that when fire should be set in one part it would immediately spread every where, and set the whole mass in flames at once. They towed this ship, on a windy day, near to the enemy's works, and on the side from which the wind was blowing. They then put it in motion toward the pier at a point where there was the greatest collection of engines and machines, and when they had got as near as they dared to go themselves, the men who were on board set the trains on fire, and made their escape in boats. The flames ran all over the vessel with inconceivable rapidity. The vessel itself drifted down upon Alexander's works, notwithstanding the most strenuous exertions of his soldiers to keep it away. The frames and engines, and the enormous and complicated machines which had been erected, took fire, and the whole mass was soon enveloped in a general conflagration.

THE SIEGE OF TYRE

The men made desperate attempts to defend their works, but all in vain. Some were killed by arrows and darts, some were burned to death, and others, in the confusion, fell into the sea. Finally, the army was obliged to draw back, and to abandon all that was combustible in the vast construction they had reared, to the devouring flames.

Not long after this the sea itself came to the aid of the Tyrians. There was a storm; and, as a consequence of it, a heavy swell rolled in from the offing, which soon undermined and washed away a large part of the pier. The effects of a heavy sea on the most massive and substantial structures, when they are fairly exposed to its impulse, are far greater than would be conceived possible by those who had not witnessed them. The most ponderous stones are removed, the strongest fastenings are torn asunder, and embankments the most compact and solid are undermined and washed away. The storm, in this case, destroyed in a few hours the work of many months, while the army of Alexander looked on from the shore witnessing its ravages in dismay.

When the storm was over, and the first shock of chagrin and disappointment had passed from the minds of the men, Alexander prepared to resume the work with fresh vigor and energy. The men commenced repairing the pier and widening it, so as to increase its strength and capacity. They dragged whole trees to the edges of it, and sunk them, branches and all, to the bottom, to form a sort of platform there, to prevent the stones from sinking into the slime. They built new towers and engines, covering them with green hides to make them fire-proof; and thus they were soon advancing again, and gradually drawing nearer to the city, and in a more threatening and formidable manner than ever.

Alexander, finding that his efforts were impeded very much by the ships of the Tyrians, determined on collecting and equipping a fleet of his own. This he did at Sidon, which was a town a short distance north of Tyre. He embarked on board this fleet himself, and came down with it into the Tyrian seas. With this fleet he had various success. He chained many of the ships together, two and two, at a little distance apart, covering the inclosed space with a platform, on which the soldiers could stand to fight. The men also erected engines on these platforms to attack the city. These engines were of various kinds. There was what they called the battering ram, which was a long and very heavy beam of wood, headed with iron or brass. This beam was suspended by a chain in the middle, so that it could be swung back and forth by the soldiers, its head striking against the wall each time, by which means the wall would sometimes be soon battered down. They had also machines for throwing great stones, or beams of wood, by means of the elastic force of strong bars of wood, or of steel, or that of twisted ropes. The part of the machine upon which the stone was placed would be drawn back by the united strength of many of the soldiers, and then, as it recovered itself when released, the stone would be thrown off into the air with prodigious velocity and force.

Alexander's double galleys answered very well as long as the water was smooth; but sometimes, when they were caught out in a swell, the rolling of the waves would rack and twist them so as to tear the platforms asunder, and sink the men in the sea. Thus difficulties unexpected and formidable were continually arising. Alexander, however, persevered through them all. The Tyrians, finding themselves pressed more and more, and seeing that the dangers impending became more and more formidable every day, at length concluded to send a great number of the women and children away to Carthage, which was a great commercial city in Africa. They were determined not to submit to Alexander, but to carry their resistance to the very last extremity. And as the closing scenes of a siege, especially if the place is at last taken by storm, are awful beyond description, they wished to save their wives, and daughters, and helpless babes from having to witness them.

In the mean time, as the siege advanced, the parties became more and more incensed against each other. They treated the captives which they took on either side with greater and greater cruelty, each thinking that they were only retaliating worse injuries from the other. The Macedonians approached nearer and nearer. The resources of the unhappy city were gradually cut off and its strength worn away. The engines approached nearer and nearer to the walls, until the battering rams bore directly upon them, and breaches began to be made. At length one great breach on the southern side was found to be "practicable," as they call it. Alexander began to prepare for the final assault, and the Tyrians saw before them the horrible prospect of being taken by storm.

Still they would not submit. Submission would now have done but little good, though it might have saved some of the final horrors of the scene. Alexander had become greatly exasperated by the long resistance which the Tyrians had made. They probably could not now have averted destruction, but they might, perhaps, have prevented its coming upon them in so terrible a shape as the irruption of thirty thousand frantic and infuriated soldiers through the breaches in their walls to take their city by storm.

The breach by which Alexander proposed to force his entrance was on the southern side. He prepared a number of ships, with platforms raised upon them in such a manner that, on getting near the walls, they could be let down, and form a sort of bridge, over which the men could pass to the broken fragments of the wall, and thence ascend through the breach above.

The plan succeeded. The ships advanced to the proposed place of landing. The bridges were let down. The men crowded over them to the foot of the wall. They clambered up through the breach to the battlements above, although the Tyrians thronged the passage and made the most desperate resistance. Hundreds were killed by darts, and arrows, and falling stones, and their bodies tumbled into the sea. The others, paying no attention to their falling comrades, and drowning the horrid screams of the crushed and the dying with their own frantic shouts of rage and fury, pressed on up the broken wall till they reached the battlements above. The vast throng then rolled along upon the top of the wall till they came to stairways and slopes by which they could descend into the city, and, pouring down through all these avenues, they spread over the streets, and satiated the hatred and rage, which had been gathering strength for seven long months, in bursting into houses, and killing and destroying all that came in their way. Thus the city was stormed.

After the soldiers were weary with the work of slaughtering the wretched inhabitants of the city, they found that many still remained alive, and Alexander tarnished the character for generosity and forbearance for which he had thus far been distinguished by the cruelty with which he treated them. Some were executed, some thrown into the sea; and it is even said that two thousand were *crucified* along the sea-shore. This may mean that their bodies were placed upon crosses after life had been destroyed by some more humane method than crucifixion. At any rate, we find frequent indications from this time that prosperity and power were beginning to exert their usual unfavorable influence upon Alexander's character. He became haughty, imperious, and cruel. He lost the modesty and gentleness which seemed to characterize him in the earlier part of his life, and began to assume the moral character, as well as perform the exploits, of a military hero.

A good illustration of this is afforded by the answer that he sent to Darius, about the time of the storming of Tyre, in reply to a second communication which he had received from him proposing terms of peace. Darius offered him a very large sum of money for the ransom of his mother, wife, and child, and agreed to give up to him all the country he had conquered, including the whole territory west of the Euphrates. He also offered him his daughter Statira in marriage. He recommended to him to accept these terms, and be content with the possessions he had already acquired; that he could not expect to succeed, if he should try, in crossing the mighty rivers of the East, which were in the way of his march toward the Persian dominions.

Alexander replied, that if he wished to marry his daughter he could do it without his consent; as to the ransom, he was not in want of money; in respect to Darius's offering to give him up all west of the Euphrates, it was absurd for a man to speak of giving what was no longer his own; that he had crossed too many seas in his military expeditions, since he left Macedon, to feel any concern about the *rivers* that he might find in his way; and that he should continue to pursue Darius wherever he might retreat in search of safety and protection, and he had no fear but that he should find and conquer him at last.

It was a harsh and cruel message to send to the unhappy monarch whom he had already so greatly injured. Parmenio advised him to accept Darius's offers. "I would," said he, "if I were Alexander." "Yes," said Alexander, "and so would I if I were Parmenio." What a reply from a youth of twenty-two to a venerable general of sixty, who had been so tried and faithful a friend, and so efficient a coadjutor both to his father and to himself, for so many years.

The siege and storming of Tyre has always been considered one of the greatest of Alexander's exploits. The boldness, the perseverance, the indomitable energy which he himself and all his army manifested, during the seven months of their Herculean toil, attracted the admiration of the world. And yet we find our feelings of sympathy for his character, and interest in his fate, somewhat alienated by the indications of pride, imperiousness, and cruelty which begin to appear. While he rises in our estimation as a military hero, he begins to sink somewhat as a man.

And yet the change was not sudden. He bore during the siege his part in the privations and difficulties which the soldiers had to endure; and the dangers to which they had to be exposed, he was always willing to share. One night he was out with a party upon the mountains. Among his few immediate attendants was Lysimachus, one of his former teachers, who always loved to accompany him at such times. Lysimachus was advanced in life, and somewhat infirm, and consequently could not keep up with the rest in the march. Alexander remained with Lysimachus, and ordered the rest to go on. The road at length became so rugged that they had to dismount from their horses and walk. Finally they lost their way, and found themselves obliged to stop for the night. They had no fire. They saw, however, at a distance, some camp fires blazing which belonged to the barbarian tribes against whom the expedition was directed. Alexander went to the nearest one. There were two men lying by it, who had been stationed to take care of it. He advanced stealthily to them and killed them both, probably while they were asleep. He then took a brand from their fire, carried it back to his own encampment, where he made a blazing fire for himself and Lysimachus, and they passed the night in comfort and safety. This is the story. How far we are to give credit to it, each reader must judge for himself. One thing is certain, however, that there are many military heroes of whom such stories would not be even fabricated.

ALEXANDER IN EGYPT

AFTER completing the subjugation of Tyre, Alexander commenced his march for Egypt. His route led him through Judea. The time was about three hundred years before the birth of Christ, and, of course, this passage of the great conqueror through the land of Israel took place between the historical periods of the Old Testament and of the New, so that no account of it is given in the sacred volume.

There was a Jewish writer named Josephus, who lived and wrote a few years after Christ, and, of course, more than three hundred years after Alexander. He wrote a history of the Jews, which is a very entertaining book to read; but he liked so much to magnify the importance of the events in the history of his country, and to embellish them with marvelous and supernatural incidents, that his narratives have not always been received with implicit faith. Josephus says that, as Alexander passed through Palestine, he went to pay a visit to Jerusalem. The circumstances of this visit, according to his account, were these.

The city of Tyre, before Alexander besieged it, as it lived entirely by commerce, and was surrounded by the sea, had to depend on the neighboring countries for a supply of food. The people were accordingly accustomed to purchase grain in Phœnicia, in Judea, and in Egypt, and transport it by their ships to the island. Alexander, in the same manner, when besieging the city, found that he must depend upon the neighboring countries for supplies of food; and he accordingly sent requisitions for such supplies to several places, and, among others, to Judea. The Jews, as Josephus says, refused to send any such supplies, saying that it would be inconsistent with fidelity to Darius, under whose government they were.

Alexander took no notice of this reply at the time, being occupied with the siege of Tyre; but, as soon as that city was taken, and he was ready to pass through Judea, he directed his march toward Jerusalem with the intention of destroying the city.

Now the chief magistrate at Jerusalem at this time, the one who had the command of the city, ruling it, of course, under a general responsibility to the Persian government, was the high priest. His name was Jaddus. In the time of Christ, about three hundred years after this, the name of the high-priest, as the reader will recollect, was Caiaphas. Jaddus and all the inhabitants of Jerusalem were very much alarmed. They knew not what to do. The siege and capture of Tyre had impressed them all with a strong sense of Alexander's terrible energy and martial power, and they began to anticipate certain destruction.

Jaddus caused great sacrifices to be offered to Almighty God, and public and solemn prayers were made, to implore his guidance and protection. The next day after these services, he told the people that they had nothing to fear. God had appeared to him in a dream, and directed him what to do. "We are not to resist the conqueror," said he, "but to go forth to meet him and welcome him. We are to strew the city with flowers, and adorn it as for a festive celebration. The priests are to be dressed in their pontifical robes and go forth, and the inhabitants are to follow them in a civic procession. In this way we are to go out to meet Alexander as he advances—and all will be well."

These directions were followed. Alexander was coming on with a full determination to destroy the city. When, however, he saw this procession, and came near enough to distinguish the appearance and dress of the high priest, he stopped, seemed surprised and pleased, and advanced toward him with an air of the profoundest deference and respect. He seemed to pay him almost religious homage and adoration. Every one was astonished. Parmenio asked him for an explanation. Alexander made the following extraordinary statement:

"When I was in Macedon, before setting out on this expedition, while I was revolving the subject in my mind, musing day after day on the means of conquering Asia, one night I had a remarkable dream. In my dream this very priest appeared before me, dressed just as he is now. He exhorted me to banish every fear, to cross the Hellespont boldly, and to push forward into the heart of Asia. He said that God would march at the head of my army, and give me the victory over all the Persians. I recognize this priest as the same person that appeared to me then. He has the same countenance, the same dress, the same stature, the same air. It is through his encouragement and aid that I am here, and I am ready to worship and adore the God whose service he administers."

Alexander joined the high priest in the procession, and they returned to Jerusalem together. There Alexander united with them and with the Jews of the city in the celebration of religious rites, by offering sacrifices and oblations in the Jewish manner. The writings which are now printed together in our Bibles, as the Old Testament, were, in those days, written separately on parchment rolls, and kept in the temple. The priests produced from the rolls the one containing the prophecies of Daniel, and they read and interpreted some of these prophecies to Alexander, which they considered to have reference to him, though written many hundred years before. Alexander was, as Josephus relates, very much pleased at the sight of these ancient predictions, and the interpretation put upon them by the priests. He assured the Jews that they should be protected in the exercise of all their rights, and especially in their religious worship, and he also promised them that he would take their brethren who resided in Media and Babylon under his special charge when he should come into possession of those places. These Jews of Media and Babylon were the descendants of captives which had been carried away from their native land in former wars.

Such is the story which Josephus relates. The Greek historians, on the other hand, make no mention of this visit to Jerusalem; and some persons think that it was never made, but that the story arose and was propagated from generation to generation among the Jews, through the influence of their desire to magnify the importance and influence of their worship, and that Josephus incorporated the account into his history without sufficiently verifying the facts.

However it may be in regard to Jerusalem, Alexander was delayed at Gaza, which, as may be seen upon the map, is on the shore of the Mediterranean Sea. It was a place of considerable commerce and wealth, and was, at this time, under the command of a governor whom Darius had stationed there. His name was Betis. Betis refused to surrender the place. Alexander stopped to besiege it, and the siege delayed him two months. He was very much exasperated at this, both against Betis and against the city.

His unreasonable anger was very much increased by a wound which he received. He was near a mound which his soldiers had been constructing near the city, to place engines upon for an attack upon the walls, when an arrow, shot from one of the engines upon the walls struck him in the breast. It penetrated his armor, and wounded him deeply in the shoulder. The wound was very painful for some time, and, the suffering which he endured from it only added fuel to the flame of his anger against the city.

At last breaches were made in the walls, and the place was taken by storm. Alexander treated the wretched captives with extreme cruelty. He cut the garrison to pieces, and sold the inhabitants to slavery. As for Betis, he dealt with him in a manner almost too horrible to be described. The reader will recollect that Achilles, at the siege of Troy, after killing Hector, dragged his dead body around the walls of the city. Alexander, growing more cruel as he became more accustomed to war and bloodshed, had been intending to imitate this example so soon as he could find an enemy worthy of such a fate. He now determined to carry his plan into execution with Betis. He ordered him into his presence. A few years before, he would have rewarded him for his fidelity in his master's service; but now, grown selfish, hard hearted, and revengeful, he looked upon him with a countenance full of vindictive exultation, and said,

"You are not going to die the simple death that you desire. You have got the worst torments that revenge can invent to suffer."

Betis did not reply, but looked upon Alexander with a calm, and composed, and unsubdued air, which incensed the conqueror more and more.

"Observe his dumb arrogance," said Alexander; "but I will conquer him. I will show him that I can draw groans from him, if nothing else."

He then ordered holes to be made through the heels of his unhappy captive, and, passing a rope through them, had the body fastened to a chariot, and dragged about the city till no life remained.

Alexander found many rich treasures in Gaza. He sent a large part of them to his mother Olympias, whom he had left in Macedon. Alexander's affection for his mother seems to have been more permanent than almost any other good trait in his character. He found, in addition to other stores of valuable merchandise, a large quantity of frankincense and myrrh. These are gums which were brought from Arabia, and were very costly. They were used chiefly in making offerings and in burning incense to the gods.

When Alexander was a young man in Macedon, before his father's death, he was one day present at the offering of sacrifices, and one of his teachers and guardians, named Leonnatus, who was standing by, thought he was rather profuse in his consumption of frankincense and myrrh. He was taking it up by handfuls and throwing it upon the fire. Leonnatus reproved him for this extravagance, and told him that when he became master of the countries where these costly gums were procured, he might be as prodigal of them as he pleased, but that in the mean time it would be proper for him to be more prudent and economical. Alexander remembered this reproof, and, finding vast stores of these expensive gums in Gaza, he sent the whole quantity to Leonnatus, telling him that he sent him this abundant supply that he might not have occasion to be so reserved and sparing for the future in his sacrifices to the gods.

After this conquest and destruction of Gaza, Alexander continued his march southward to the frontiers of Egypt. He reached these frontiers at the city of Pelusium. The Egyptians had been under the Persian dominion, but they abhorred it, and were very ready to submit to Alexander's sway. They sent embassadors to meet him upon the frontiers. The governors of the cities, as he advanced into the country, finding that it would be useless to resist, and warned by the terrible example of Thebes, Tyre, and Gaza, surrendered to him as fast as he summoned them.

He went to Memphis. Memphis was a great and powerful city, situated in what was called Lower Egypt, on the Nile, just above where the branches which form the mouths of the Nile separate from the main stream. All that part of Egypt is flat country, having been formed by the deposits brought down by the Nile. Such land is called *alluvial;* it is always level, and, as it consists of successive deposits from the turbid waters of the river, made in the successive inundations, it forms always a very rich soil, deep and inexhaustible, and is, of course, extremely fertile. Egypt has been celebrated for its unexampled fertility from the earliest times. It waves with fields of corn and grain, and is adorned with groves of the most luxuriant growth and richest verdure.

It is only, however, so far as the land is formed by the deposits of the Nile, that this scene of verdure and beauty extends. On the east it is bounded by ranges of barren and rocky hills, and on the west by vast deserts, consisting of moving sands, from which no animal or vegetable life can derive the means of existence. The reason of this sterility seems to be the absence of water. The geological formation of the land is such that it furnishes few springs of water, and no streams, and in that climate it seldom or never rains. If there is water, the most barren sands will clothe themselves with some species of vegetation, which, in its decay, will form a soil that will nourish more and more fully each succeeding generation of plants. But in the absence of water, any surface of earth will soon become a barren sand. The wind will drive away every thing imponderable, leaving only the heavy sands, to drift in storms, like fields of snow.

Among these African deserts, however, there are some fertile spots. They are occasioned by springs which arise in little dells, and which saturate the ground with moisture for some distance around them. The water from these springs flows for some distance, in many cases, in a little stream, before it is finally lost and absorbed in the sands. The whole tract under the influence of this irrigation clothes itself with verdure. Trees grow up to shade it. It forms a spot whose beauty, absolutely great, is heightened by the contrast which it presents to the gloomy and desolate desert by which it is surrounded. Such a green spot in the desert is called an Oasis. They are the resort and the refuge of the traveler and the pilgrim, who seek shelter and repose upon them in their weary journeys over the trackless wilds.

Nor must it be supposed that these islands of fertility and verdure are always *small*. Some of them are very extensive, and contain a considerable population. There is one called the Great Oasis, which consists of a chain of fertile tracts of about a hundred miles in length. Another, called the Oasis of Siwah, has, in modern times, a population of eight thousand souls. This last is situated not far from the shores of the Mediterranean Sea—at least not very far: perhaps two or three hundred miles—and it was a very celebrated spot in Alexander's day.

The cause of its celebrity was that it was the seat and center of the worship of a famous deity called Jupiter Ammon. This god was said to be the son of Jupiter, though there were all sorts of stories about his origin and early history. He had the form of a ram, and was worshiped by the people of Egypt, and also by the Carthaginians, and by the people of Northern Africa generally. His temple was in this Oasis, and it was surrounded by a considerable population, which was supported, in a great degree, by the expenditures of the worshipers who came as pilgrims, or otherwise, to sacrifice at his shrine.

It is said that Alexander, finding that the various objects of human ambition which he had been so rapidly attaining by his victories and conquests for the past few years were insufficient to satisfy him, began now to aspire for some supernatural honors, and he accordingly conceived the design of having himself declared to be the son of a god. The heroes of Homer were sons of the gods. Alexander envied them the fame and honor which this distinction gave them in the opinion of mankind. He determined to visit the temple of Jupiter Ammon in the Oasis of Siwah, and to have the declaration of his divine origin made by the priests there.

He proceeded, accordingly, to the mouth of the Nile, where he found a very eligible places, as he believed, for the foundation of a commercial city, and he determined to build it on his return. Thence he marched along the shores of the Mediterranean, toward the west, until he reached a place called Parætonium, which will be found upon the map. He then left the sea-shore and marched south, striking at once into the desert when he left the sea. He was accompanied by a small detachment of his army as an escort, and they journeyed eleven days before they reached the Oasis.

They had a variety of perilous adventures in crossing the desert. For the first two days the soldiers were excited and pleased with the novelty and romantic grandeur of the scene. The desert has, in some degree, the sublimity of the ocean. There is the same boundless expanse, the same vast, unbroken curve of the horizon, the same tracklessness, the same solitude. There is, in addition, a certain profound and awful stillness and repose, which imparts to it a new element of impressiveness and grandeur. Its dread and solemn silence is far more imposing and sublime than the loudest thunders of the seas.

The third day the soldiers began to be weary of such a march. They seemed afraid to penetrate any further into such boundless and terrible solitudes. They had been obliged to bring water with them in goat-skins, which were carried by camels. The camel is the only beast of burden which can be employed upon the deserts. There is a peculiarity in the anatomical structure of this animal by which he can take in, at one time, a supply of water for many days. He is formed, in fact, for the desert. In his native state he lives in the oases and in the valleys. He eats the herbage which grows among the rocks and hills that alternate with the great sandy plains in all these countries. In passing from one of his scanty pasturages to another, he has long journeys to make across the sands, where, though he can find food here and there, there is no water. Providence has formed him with a structure adapted to this exigency, and by means of it he becomes extremely useful to man.

The soldiers of Alexander did not take a sufficient supply of water, and were reduced, at one time, to great distress. They were relieved, the story says, by a rain, though rain is extremely unusual in the deserts. Alexander attributed this supply to the miraculous interposition of Heaven. They catch the rain, in such cases, with cloths, and afterward wring out the water; though in this instance, as the historians of that day say, the soldiers did not wait for this tardy method of supply, but the whole detachment held back their heads and opened their mouths, to catch the drops of rain as they fell.

There was another danger to which they were exposed in their march, more terrible even than the scarcity of water. It was that of being overwhelmed in the clouds of sand and dust which sometimes swept over the desert in gales of wind. These were called sand-storms. The fine sand flew, in such cases, in driving clouds, which filled the eyes and stopped the breath of the traveler, and finally buried his body under its drifts when he laid down to die. A large army of fifty thousand men, under a former Persian king, had been overwhelmed and destroyed in this way, some years before, in some of the Egyptian deserts. Alexander's soldiers had heard of this calamity, and they were threatened sometimes with the same fate. They, however, at length escaped all the dangers of the desert, and began to approach the green and fertile land of the Oasis.

The change from the barren and dismal loneliness of the sandy plains to the groves and the villages, the beauty and the verdure of the Oasis, was delightful both to Alexander himself and to all his men. The priests at the great temple of Jupiter Ammon received them all with marks of great distinction and honor. The most solemn and magnificent ceremonies were performed, with offerings, oblations, and sacrifices. The priests, after conferring in secret with the god in the temple, came out with the annunciation that Alexander was indeed his son, and they paid him, accordingly, almost divine honors. He is supposed to have bribed them to do this by presents and pay. Alexander returned at length to Memphis, and in all his subsequent orders and decrees he styled himself Alexander king, son of Jupiter Ammon.

But, though Alexander was thus willing to impress his ignorant soldiers with a mysterious veneration for his fictitious divinity, he was not deceived himself on the subject; he sometimes even made his pretensions to the divine character a subject of joke. For instance, they one day brought him in too little fire in the *focus*. The focus, or fireplace used in Alexander's day was a small metallic stand, on which the fire was built. It was placed wherever convenient in the tent, and the smoke escaped above. They had put upon the focus too little fuel one day when they brought it in. Alexander asked the officer to let him have either some wood or some frankincense; they might consider him, he said, as a god or as a man, whichever they pleased, but he wished to be treated either like one or the other.

On his return from the Oasis Alexander carried forward his plan of building a city at the mouth of the Nile. He drew the plan, it is said, with his own hands. He superintended the constructions, and invited artisans and mechanics from all nations to come and reside in it. They accepted the invitation in great numbers, and the city soon became large, and wealthy, and powerful. It was intended as a commercial post, and the wisdom and sagacity which Alexander manifested in the selection of the site is shown by the fact that the city rose immediately to the rank of the great seat of trade and commerce for all those shores, and has continued to hold that rank now for twenty centuries.

A FOCUS

There was an island near the coast, opposite the city, called the island of Pharos. They built a most magnificent light-house upon one extremity of this island, which was considered, in those days, one of the wonders of the world. It was said to be five hundred feet high. This may have been an exaggeration. At any rate, it was celebrated throughout the world in its day, and its existence and its greatness made an impression on the human mind which has not yet been effaced. Pharos is the name for light-house, in many languages, to the present day.

In building the city of Alexandria, Alexander laid aside, for a time, his natural and proper character, and assumed a mode of action in strong contrast with the ordinary course of his life. He was, throughout most of his career, a destroyer. He roamed over the world to interrupt commerce, to break in upon and disturb the peaceful pursuits of industry, to batter down city walls, and burn dwellings, and kill men. This is the true vocation of a hero and a conqueror; but at the mouth of the

Nile Alexander laid aside this character. He turned his energies to the work of planning means to do good. He constructed a port; he built warehouses; he provided accommodations and protection for merchants and artisans. The nations exchanged their commodities far more easily and extensively in consequence of these facilities, and the means of comfort and enjoyment were multiplied and increased in thousands and thousands of huts in the great cities of Egypt, and in the rural districts along the banks of the Nile. The good, too, which he thus commenced, has perpetuated itself. Alexandria has continued to fulfill its beneficent function for two thousand years. It is the only monument of his greatness which remains. Every thing else which he accomplished perished when he died. How much better would it have been for the happiness of mankind, as well as for his own true fame and glory, if doing good had been the rule of his life instead of the exception.

THE GREAT VICTORY

A ll this time, however, he was very far from being satisfied, or feeling that his work was done. Darius, whom he considered his great enemy, was still in the field unsubdued. He had retreated across the Euphrates, and was employed in assembling a vast collection of forces from all the Eastern nations which were under his sway, to meet Alexander in the final contest. Alexander therefore made arrangements at Tyre for the proper government of the various kingdoms and provinces which he had already conquered, and then began to prepare for marching eastward with the main body of his army.

During all this time the ladies of Darius's family, who had been taken captive at Issus, had been retained in captivity, and made to accompany Alexander's army in its marches. Alexander refused to accede to any of the plans and propositions which Darius made and offered for the redemption of his wife and mother, but insisted on retaining them as his prisoners. He, however, treated them with respect and high consideration. He provided them with royal tents of great magnificence, and had them conveyed from place to place, when his army moved, with all the royal state to which they had been accustomed when in the court of Darius.

It has been generally thought a proof of nobleness of spirit and generosity in Alexander that he treated his captives in this manner. It would seem, however, that true generosity would have prompted the restoration of these unhappy and harmless prisoners to the husband and father who mourned their separation from him, and their cruel sufferings, with bitter grief. It is more probable, therefore, that policy, and a regard for his own aggrandizement, rather than compassion for the suffering, led him to honor his captive queens. It was a great glory to him, in a martial point of view, to have such trophies of his victory in his train; and, of course, the more highly he honored the personages, the more glorious the trophy appeared. Accordingly, Alexander did every thing in his power to magnify the importance of his royal captives, by the splendor of their retinue, and the pomp and pageantry with which he invested their movements.

A short time after leaving Tyre, on the march eastward, Statira, the wife of Darius, was taken suddenly ill and died. The tidings were immediately brought to Alexander, and he repaired without delay to Sysigambis's tent. Sysigambis was the mother of Darius. She was in the greatest agony of grief. She was lying upon the floor of her tent, surrounded by the ladies of her court, and entirely overwhelmed with sorrow. Alexander did all in his power to calm and comfort her.

One of the officers of Queen Statira's household made his escape from the camp immediately after his mistress's death, and fled across the country to Darius, to carry him the heavy tidings. Darius was overwhelmed with affliction. The officer, however, in farther interviews, gave him such an account of the kind and respectful treatment which the ladies had received from Alexander, during all the time of their captivity, as greatly to relieve his mind, and to afford him a high degree of comfort and consolation. He expressed a very strong sense of gratitude to Alexander for his generosity and kindness, and said that if his kingdom of Persia *must* be conquered, he sincerely wished that it might fall into the hands of such a conqueror as Alexander.

By looking at the map at the commencement of the volume, it will be seen that the Tigris and the Euphrates are parallel streams, flowing through the heart of the western part of Asia toward the southeast, and emptying into the Persian Gulf. The country between these two rivers, which was extremely populous and fertile, was called Mesopotamia. Darius had collected an immense army here. The various detachments filled all the plains of Mesopotamia. Alexander turned his course a little northward, intending to pass the River Euphrates at a famous ancient crossing at Thapsacus, which may be seen upon the map. When he arrived at this place he found a small Persian army there. They, however, retired as he approached. Alexander built two bridges across the river, and passed his army safely over.

In the mean time, Darius, with his enormous host, passed across the Tigris, and moved toward the northward, along the eastern side of the river. He had to cross the various branches of the Tigris as he advanced. At one of them, called the Lycus, which may also be seen upon the map, there was a bridge. It took the vast host which Darius had collected *five days* to pass this bridge.

While Darius had been thus advancing to the northward into the latitude where he knew that Alexander must cross the rivers, Alexander himself, and his small but compact and fearless body of Grecian troops, were moving eastward, toward the same region to which Darius's line of march was tending. Alexander at length reached the Tigris. He was obliged to ford this stream. The banks were steep and the current was rapid, and the men were in great danger of being swept away. To prevent this danger, the ranks, as they advanced, linked their arms together, so that each man might be sustained by his comrades. They held their shields above their heads to keep them from the water. Alexander waded like the rest, though he kept in front, and reached the bank before the others. Standing there, he indicated to the advancing column, by gesticulation, where to land, the noise of the water being too great to allow his voice to be heard. To see him standing there, safely landed, and with an expression of confidence and triumph in his attitude and air, awakened fresh energy in the heart of every soldier in the columns which were crossing the stream.

Notwithstanding this encouragement, however, the passage of the troops and the landing on the bank produced a scene of great confusion. Many of the soldiers had tied up a portion of their clothes in bundles, which they held above their heads, together with their arms, as they waded along through the swift current of the stream. They, however, found it impossible to carry these bundles, but had to abandon them at last in order to save themselves, as they staggered along through deep and rapid water, and over a concealed bottom of slippery stones. Thousands of these bundles, mingled with spears, darts, and every other sort of weapon that would float, were swept down by the current, to impede and embarrass the men who were passing below.

At length, however, the men themselves succeeded in getting over in safety, though a large quantity of arms and of clothing was lost. There was no enemy upon the bank to oppose them. Darius could not, in fact, well meet and oppose Alexander in his attempt to cross the river, because he could not determine at what point he would probably make the attempt, in season to concentrate so large an army to oppose him. Alexander's troops, being a comparatively small and compact body, and being accustomed to move with great promptness and celerity, could easily evade any attempt of such an unwieldy mass of forces to oppose his crossing at any particular point upon the stream. At any rate, Darius did not make any such attempt, and Alexander had no difficulties to encounter in crossing the Tigris other than the physical obstacles presented by the current of the stream.

Darius's plan was, therefore, not to intercept Alexander on his march, but to choose some great and convenient battle-field, where he could collect his forces, and marshal them advantageously and so await an attack there. He knew very well that his enemy would seek him out, wherever he was, and, consequently, that he might choose his position. He found such a field in an extensive plain at Guagamela, not far from the city of Arbela. The spot has received historical immortality under the name of the plain of Arbela.

Darius was several days in concentrating his vast armies upon this plain. He constructed encampments; he leveled the inequalities which would interfere with the movements of his great bodies of cavalry; he guarded the approaches, too, as much as possible. There is a little instrument used in war called a *caltrop*. It consists of a small ball of iron, with several sharp points projecting from it one or two inches each way. If these instruments are thrown upon the ground at random, one of the points must necessarily be upward, and the horses that tread upon them are lamed and disabled at once. Darius caused caltrops to be scattered in the grass and along the roads, wherever the army of Alexander would be likely to approach his troops on the field of battle.

Alexander, having crossed the river, encamped for a day or two on the banks, to rest and refresh, and to rearrange his army. While here, the soldiers were one night thrown into consternation by an eclipse of the moon. Whenever an eclipse of the moon takes place, it is, of course, when the moon is full, so that the eclipse is always a sudden, and, among an ignorant people, an unexpected waning of the orb in the height of its splendor; and as such people know not the cause of the phenomenon, they are often extremely terrified. Alexander's soldiers were thrown into consternation by the eclipse. They considered it the manifestation of the displeasure of Heaven at their presumptuous daring in crossing such rivers, and penetrating to such a distance to invade the territories of another king.

In fact, the men were predisposed to fear. Having wandered to a vast distance from home, having passed over such mountains and deserts, and now, at last, having crossed a deep and dangerous river, and thrown themselves into the immediate vicinity of a foe ten times as numerous as themselves, it was natural that they should feel some misgivings. And when, at night, impressed with the sense of solemnity which night always imparts to strange and novel scenes, they looked up to the bright round moon, pleased with the expression of cheerfulness and companionship which beams always in her light, to find her suddenly waning, changing her form, withdrawing her bright beams, and looking down upon them with a lurid and murky light, it was not surprising that they felt an emotion of terror. In fact, there is always an element of terror in the emotion excited by looking upon an eclipse, which an instinctive feeling of the heart inspires. It invests the spectacle with a solemn grandeur. It holds the spectator, however cultivated and refined, in silence while he gazes at it. It mingles with a scientific appreciation of the vastness of the movements and magnitudes by which the effect is produced, and while the one occupies the intellect, the other impresses the soul. The mind that has lost, through its philosophy, the power of feeling this emotion of awe in such scenes, has sunk, not risen. Its possessor has made himself inferior, not superior, to the rest of his species, by having paralyzed one of his susceptibilities of pleasure. To him an eclipse is only curious and wonderful; to others it is sublime.

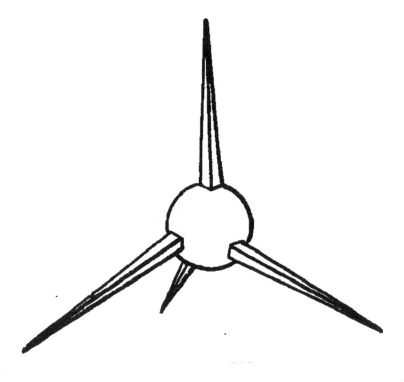

THE CALTROP

The soldiers of Alexander were extremely terrified. A great panic spread throughout the encampment. Alexander himself, instead of attempting to allay their fears by reasoning, or treating them as of no importance, immediately gave the subject his most serious attention. He called together the soothsayers, and directed them to consult together, and let him know what this great phenomenon portended. This mere committing of the subject to the attention of the soothsayers had a great effect among all the soldiers of the army. It calmed them. It changed their agitation and terror into a feeling of suspense, in awaiting the answer of the soothsayers, which was far less painful and dangerous; and at length, when the answer came, it allayed their anxiety and fear altogether. The soothsayers said that the sun was on Alexander's side, and the moon on that of the Persians, and that this sudden waning of her light foreshadowed the defeat and destruction which the Persians were about to undergo. The army were satisfied with this decision, and were inspired with new confidence and ardor. It is often idle to attempt to oppose ignorance and absurdity by such feeble instruments as truth and reason, and the wisest managers of mankind have generally been most successful when their plan has been to counteract one folly by means of the influence of another.

Alexander's army consisted of about fifty thousand men, with the phalanx in the center. This army moved along down the eastern bank of the Tigris, the scouts pressing forward as far as possible in every direction in front of the main army, in order to get intelligence of the foe. It is in this way that two great armies *feel* after each other, as it were, like insects creeping over the ground, exploring the way before them with their *antennæ*. At length, after three days' advance, the scouts came in with intelligence of the enemy. Alexander pressed forward with a detachment of his army to meet them. They proved to be, however, not the main body of Darius's army, but only a single corps of a thousand men, in advance of the rest. They retreated as Alexander approached. He, however, succeeded in capturing some horsemen, who gave the information that Darius had assembled his vast forces on the plain of Arbela, and was waiting there in readiness to give his advancing enemy battle.

Alexander halted his troops. He formed an encampment, and made arrangements for depositing his baggage there. He refreshed the men, examined and repaired their arms, and made the arrangements for battle. These operations consumed several days. At the end of that time, early one morning, long before day, the camp was in motion, and the columns, armed and equipped for immediate contest, moved forward.

They expected to have reached the camp of Darius at daybreak, but the distance was greater than they had supposed. At length, however, the Macedonians, in their march, came upon the brow of a range of hills, from which they looked down upon numberless and endless lines of infantry and cavalry, and ranges after ranges of tents, which filled the plain. Here the army paused while Alexander examined the field, studying for a long time, and with great attention, the numbers and disposition of the enemy. They were four miles distant still, but the murmuring sounds of their voices and movements came to the ears of the Macedonians through the calm autumnal air.

Alexander called the leading officers together, and held a consultation on the question whether to march down and attack the Persians on the plain that night, or to wait till the next day. Parmenio was in favor of a night attack, in order to surprise the enemy by coming upon them at an unexpected time. But Alexander said no. He was sure of victory. He had got his enemies all before him; they were fully in his power. He would, therefore, take no advantage but would attack them fairly and in open day. Alexander had fifty thousand men; the Persians were variously estimated between five hundred thousand and a million. There is something sublime in the idea of such a pause, made by the Macedonian phalanx and its wings, on the slopes of the hills, suspending its attack upon ten times its number, to give the mighty mass of their enemies the chances of a fair and equal contest.

Alexander made congratulatory addresses to his soldiers on the occasion of their having now at last before them, what they had so long toiled and labored to attain, the whole concentrated force of the Persian empire. They were now going to contend, not for single provinces and kingdoms, as heretofore, but for general empire; and the victory which they were about to achieve would place them on the summit of human glory. In all that he said on the subject, the unquestionable certainty of victory was assumed.

Alexander completed his arrangements, and then retired to rest. He went to sleep—at least he appeared to do so. Early in the morning Parmenio arose, summoned the men to their posts, and arranged every thing for the march. He then went to Alexander's tent. Alexander was still asleep. He awoke him, and told him that all was ready. Parmenio expressed surprise at his sleeping so quietly at a time when such vast issues were at stake. "You seem as calm," said he, "as if you had had the battle and gained the victory." "I have done so," said Alexander. "I consider the whole work done when we have gained access to Darius and his forces, and find him ready to give us battle."

Alexander soon appeared at the head of his troops. Of course this day was one of the most important ones of his life, and one of the historians of the time has preserved an account of his dress as he went into battle. He wore a short tunic, girt close around him, and over it a linen breast-plate, strongly quilted. The belt by which the tunic was held was embossed with figures of beautiful workmanship. This belt was a present to him from some of the people of the conquered countries through which he had passed, and it was very much admired. He had a helmet upon his head, of polished steel, with a neck piece, also of steel, ornamented with precious stones. His helmet was surmounted with a white plume. His sword, which was a present to him from the King of Cyprus, was very light and slender, and of the most perfect temper. He carried, also, a shield and a lance, made in the best possible manner for use, not for display. Thus his dress corresponded with the character of his action. It was simple, compact, and whatever of value it possessed consisted in those substantial excellences which would give the bearer the greatest efficiency on the field of battle.

The Persians were accustomed to make use of elephants in their wars. They also had chariots, with scythes placed at the axles, which they were accustomed to drive among their enemies and mow them down. Alexander resorted to none of these contrivances. There was the phalanx—the terrible phalanx—advancing irresistibly either in one body or in detachments, with columns of infantry and flying troops of horsemen on the wings. Alexander relied simply on the strength, the courage, the energy, and the calm and steady, but resistless ardor of his men, arranging them in simple combinations, and leading them forward directly to their work.

The Macedonians cut their way through the mighty mass of their enemies with irresistible force. The elephants turned and fled. The foot soldiers seized the horses of some of the scythe-armed chariots and cut the traces. In respect to others, they opened to the right and left and let them pass through, when they were easily captured by the men in the rear. In the mean time the phalanx pressed on, enjoying a great advantage in the level nature of the ground. The Persian troops were broken in upon and driven away wherever they were attacked. In a word, before night the whole mighty mass was scattering every where in confusion, except some hundreds of thousands left trampled upon and dead, or else writhing upon the ground, and groaning in their dying agonies. Darius himself fled. Alexander pursued him with a troop of horse as far as Arbela, which had been Darius's head-quarters, and where he had deposited immense treasures. Darius had gone through and escaped when Alexander arrived at Arbela, but the city and the treasures fell into Alexander's hands.

Although Alexander had been so completely victorious over his enemies on the day of battle, and had maintained his ground against them with such invincible power, he was, nevertheless, a few days afterward, driven entirely off the field, and completely away from the region where the battle had been fought. What the living men, standing erect in arms, and full of martial vigor, could not do, was easily and effectually accomplished by their dead bodies corrupting on the plain. The corpses of three hundred thousand men, and an equal bulk of the bodies of elephants and horses, was too enormous a mass to be buried. It had to be abandoned; and the horrible effluvia and pestilence which it emitted drove all the inhabitants of the country away. Alexander marched his troops rapidly off the ground, leaving, as the direct result of the battle, a wide extent of country depopulated and desolate, with this vast mass of putrefaction and pestilence reigning in awful silence and solitude in the midst of it.

Alexander went to Babylon. The governor of the city prepared to receive him as a conqueror. The people came out in throngs to meet him, and all the avenues of approach were crowded with spectators. All the city walls, too, were covered with men and women, assembled to witness the scene. As for Alexander himself, he was filled with pride and pleasure at thus arriving at the full accomplishment of his earliest and long-cherished dreams of glory.

The great store-house of the royal treasures of Persia was at Susa, a strong city east of Babylon. Susa was the winter residence of the Persian kings, as Ecbatana, further north, among the mountains, was their summer residence. There was a magnificent palace and a very strong citadel at Susa, and the treasures were kept in the citadel. It is said that in times of peace the Persian monarchs had been accustomed to collect coin, melt it down, and cast the gold in earthen jars. The jars were afterward broken off from the gold, leaving the bullion in the form of the interior of the jars. An enormous amount of gold and silver, and of other treasures, had been thus collected. Alexander was aware of this depository before he advanced to meet Darius, and, on the day of the battle of Arbela, as soon as the victory was decided, he sent an officer from the very field to summon Susa to surrender. They obeyed the summons, and Alexander, soon after his great public entrance into Babylon, marched to Susa, and took possession of the vast stores of wealth accumulated there. The amount was enormous, both in quantity and value, and the seizing of it was a very magnificent act of plunder. In fact, it is probable that Alexander's slaughter of the Persian army at Arbela, and subsequent spoilation of Susa, constitute, taken together, the most gigantic case of murder and robbery which was ever committed by man; so that, in performing these deeds, the great hero attained at last to the glory of having perpetrated the grandest and most imposing of all human crimes. That these deeds were really crimes there can be no doubt, when we consider that Alexander did not pretend to have any other motive in this invasion than love of conquest, which is, in other words, love of violence and plunder. They are only technically shielded from being called crimes by the fact that the earth has no laws and no tribunals high enough to condemn such enormous burglaries as that of one quarter of the globe breaking violently and murderously in upon and robbing the other.

Besides the treasures, Alexander found also at Susa a number of trophies which had been brought by Xerxes from Greece; for Xerxes had invaded Greece some hundred years before Alexander's day, and had brought to Susa the spoils and the trophies of his victories. Alexander sent them all back to Greece again.

From Susa the conqueror moved on to Persepolis, the great Persian capital. On his march he had to pass through a defile of the mountains. The mountaineers had been accustomed to exact tribute here of all who passed, having a sort of right, derived from ancient usage, to the payment of a toll. They sent to Alexander when they heard that he was approaching, and informed him that he could not pass with his army without paying the customary toll. Alexander sent back word that he would meet them at the pass, and give them *their due*.

ALEXANDER AT THE PASS OF SUSA

They understood this, and prepared to defend the pass. Some Persian troops joined them. They built walls and barricades across the narrow passages. They collected great stones on the brinks of precipices, and on the declivities of the mountains, to roll down upon the heads of their enemies. By these and every other means they attempted to stop Alexander's passage. But he had contrived to send detachments around by circuitous and precipitous paths, which even the mountaineers had deemed impracticable, and thus attack his enemies suddenly and unexpectedly from above their own positions. As usual, his plan succeeded. The mountaineers were driven away, and the conqueror advanced toward the great Persian capital.

THE DEATH OF DARIUS

ALEXANDER'S march from Susa to Persepolis was less a march than a triumphal progress. He felt the pride and elation so naturally resulting from success very strongly. The moderation and forbearance which had characterized him in his earlier years, gradually disappeared as he became great and powerful. He was intoxicated with his success. He became haughty, vain, capricious, and cruel. As he approached Persepolis, he conceived the idea that, as this city was the capital and center of the Persian monarchy, and, as such, the point from which had emanated all the Persian hostility to Greece, he owed it some signal retribution. Accordingly, although the inhabitants made no opposition to his entrance, he marched in with the phalanx formed, and gave the soldiers liberty to kill and plunder as they pleased.

There was another very striking instance of the capricious recklessness now beginning to appear in Alexander's character, which occurred soon after he had taken possession of Persepolis. He was giving a great banquet to his friends, the officers of the army, and to Persians of distinction among those who had submitted to him. There was, among other women at this banquet, a very beautiful and accomplished female named Thais. Alexander made her his favorite and companion, though she was not his wife. Thais did all in her power to captivate and please Alexander during the feast by her vivacity, her wit, her adroit attentions to him, and the display of her charms, and at length, when he himself, as well as the other guests, were excited with wine, she asked him to allow her to have the pleasure of going herself and setting fire, with her own hands, to the great palace of the Persian kings in the city. Thais was a native of Attica in Greece, a kingdom of which Athens was the capital. Xerxes, who had built the great palace of Persepolis, had formerly invaded Greece and had burned Athens, and now Thais desired to burn his palace in Persepolis, to gratify her

revenge, by making, of its conflagration an evening spectacle to enter-
tain the Macedonian party after their supper. Alexander agreed to the
proposal, and the whole company moved forward. Taking the torches
from the banqueting halls, they sallied forth, alarming the city with
their shouts, and with the flashing of the lights they bore. The plan of
Thais was carried fully into effect, every half-intoxicated guest assist-
ing, by putting fire to the immense pile wherever they could get access
to it. They performed the barbarous deed with shouts of vengeance and
exultation.

There is, however, something very solemn and awful in a great
conflagration at night, and very few incendiaries can gaze upon the
fury of the lurid and frightful flames which they have caused to ascend
without some misgivings and some remorse. Alexander was sobered
by the grand and sublime, but terrible spectacle. He was awed by it.
He repented. He ordered the fire to be extinguished; but it was too late.
The palace was destroyed, and one new blot, which has never since
been effaced, was cast upon Alexander's character and fame.

And yet, notwithstanding these increasing proofs of pride and cruelty, which were beginning to be developed, Alexander still preserved
some of the early traits of character which had made him so great a
favorite in the commencement of his career. He loved his mother, and
lent her presents continually from the treasures which were falling all
the time into his possession. She was a woman of a proud, imperious,
and ungovernable character, and she made Antipater, whom Alexander
had left in command in Macedon, infinite trouble. She wanted to exercise the powers of government herself, and was continually urging
this. Alexander would not comply with these wishes, but he paid her
personally every attention in his power, and bore all her invectives and
reproaches with great patience and good humor. At one time he received a long letter from Antipater, full of complaints against her; but
Alexander, after reading it, said that they were heavy charges it was
true, but that a single one of his mother's tears would outweigh ten
thousand such accusations.

Olympias used to write very frequently to Alexander, and in these
letters she would criticise and discuss his proceedings, and make
comments upon the characters and actions of his generals. Alexander
kept these letters very secret, never showing them to any one. One day,
however, when he was reading one of these letters, Hephæstion, the
personal friend and companion who has been already several times
mentioned, came up, half playfully, and began to took over his shoulder. Alexander went on, allowing him to read, and then, when the

letter was finished he took the signet ring from his finger and pressed it upon Hephæstion's lips, a signal for silence and secrecy.

Alexander was very kind to Sysigambis, the mother of Darius, and also to Darius's children. He would not give these unhappy captives their liberty, but in every other respect he treated them with the greatest possible kindness and consideration. He called Sysigambis mother, loaded her with presents—presents, it is true, which he had plundered from her son, but to which it was considered, in those days, that he had acquired a just and perfect title. When he reached Susa, he established Sysigambis and the children there in great state. This had been their usual residence in most seasons of the year, when not at Persepolis, so that here they were, as it were, at home. Ecbatana was, as has been already mentioned, further north, among the mountains. After the battle of Arbela, while Alexander marched to Babylon and to Susa, Darius had fled to Ecbatana, and was now there, his family being thus at one of the royal palaces under the command of the conqueror, and he himself independent, but insecure, in the other. He had with him about forty thousand men, who still remained faithful to his fallen fortunes. Among these were several thousand Greeks, whom he had collected in Asia Minor and other Grecian countries, and whom he had attached to his service by means of pay.

He called the officers of his army together, and explained to them the determination that he had come to in respect to his future movements. "A large part of those," said he, "who formerly served as officers of my government have abandoned me in my adversity, and gone over to Alexander's side. They have surrendered to him the towns, and citadels, and provinces which I intrusted to their fidelity. You alone remain faithful and true. As for myself, I might yield to the conqueror, and have him assign to me some province or kingdom to govern as his subordinate; but I will never submit to such a degradation. I can die in the struggle, but never will yield. I will wear no crown which another puts upon my brow, nor give up my right to reign over the empire of my ancestors till I give up my life. If you agree with me in this determination, let us act energetically upon it. We have it in our power to terminate the injuries we are suffering, or else to avenge them."

The army responded most cordially to this appeal. They were ready, they said, to follow him wherever he should lead. All this apparent enthusiasm, however, was very delusive and unsubstantial. A general named Bessus, combining with some other officers in the army, conceived the plan of seizing Darius and making him a prisoner, and then taking command of the army himself. If Alexander should pursue him, and be likely to overtake and conquer him, he then thought that, by giving up Darius as a prisoner, he could stipulate for liberty and safety, and perhaps great rewards, both for himself and for those who acted with him. If, on the other hand, they should succeed in increasing their own forces so as to make head against Alexander, and finally to drive him away, then Bessus was to usurp the throne, and dispose of Darius by assassinating him, or imprisoning him for life in some remote and solitary castle.

Bessus communicated his plans, very cautiously at first, to the leading officers of the army. The Greek soldiers were not included in the plot. They, however, heard and saw enough to lead them to suspect what was in preparation. They warned Darius, and urged him to rely upon them more than he had done; to make them his body-guard; and to pitch his tent in their part of the encampment. But Darius declined these proposals. He would not, he said, distrust and abandon his countrymen, who were his natural protectors, and put himself in the hands of strangers. He would not betray and desert his friends in anticipation of their deserting and betraying him.

In the mean time, as Alexander advanced toward Ecbatana, Darius and his forces retreated from it toward the eastward, through the great tract of country lying south of the Caspian Sea. There is a mountainous region here, with a defile traversing it, through which it would be necessary for Darius to pass. This defile was called the Caspian Gates, the name referring to rocks on each side. The marching of an army through a narrow and dangerous defile like this always causes detention and delay, and Alexander hastened forward in hopes to overtake Darius before he should reach it. He advanced with such speed that only the strongest and most robust of his army could keep up. Thousands, worn out with exertion and toil, were left behind, and many of the horses sank down by the road side, exhausted with heat and fatigue, to die. Alexander pressed desperately on with all who were able to follow.

It was all in vain, however; it was too late when he arrived at the pass. Darius had gone through with all his army. Alexander stopped to rest his men, and to allow time for those behind to come up. He then went on for a couple of days, when he encamped, in order to send out foraging parties—that is to say, small detachments, dispatched to explore the surrounding country in search of grain and other food for the horses. Food for the horses of an army being too bulky to be transported far, has to be collected day by day from the neighborhood of the line of march.

While halting for these foraging parties to return, a Persian nobleman came into the camp, and informed Alexander that Darius and the forces accompanying him were encamped about two days' march in advance, but that Bessus was in command—the conspiracy having been successful, and Darius having been deposed and made a prisoner. The Greeks, who had adhered to their fidelity, finding that all the army were combined against them, and that they were not strong enough to resist, had abandoned the Persian camp, and had retired to the mountains, where they were awaiting the result.

Alexander determined to set forward immediately in pursuit of Bessus and his prisoner. He did not wait for the return of the foraging parties. He selected the ablest and most active, both of foot soldiers and horsemen, ordered them to take two days' provisions, and then set forth with them that very evening. The party pressed on all that night, and the next day till noon. They halted till evening, and then set forth again. Very early the next morning they arrived at the encampment which the Persian nobleman had described. They found the remains of the camp-fires, and all the marks usually left upon a spot which has been used as the bivouac of an army. The army itself, however, was gone.

The pursuers were now too much fatigued to go any further without rest. Alexander remained here, accordingly, through the day, to give his men and his horses refreshment and repose. That night they set forward again, and the next day at noon they arrived at another encampment of the Persians, which they had left scarcely twenty-four hours before. The officers of Alexander's army were excited and animated in the highest degree, as they found themselves thus drawing so near to the great object of their pursuit. They were ready for any exertions, any privation and fatigue, any measures, however extraordinary, to accomplish their end.

Alexander inquired of the inhabitants of the place whether there were not some shorter road than the one along which the enemy were moving. There was one cross-road, but it led through a desolate and desert tract of land, destitute of water. In the march of an army, as the men are always heavily loaded with arms and provisions, and water can not be carried, it is always considered essential to choose routes which will furnish supplies of water by the way. Alexander, however, disregarded this consideration here, and prepared at once to push into the cross-road with a small detachment. He had been now two years advancing from Macedon into the heart of Asia, always in quest of Darius as his great opponent and enemy. He had conquered his armies, taken his cities, plundered his palaces, and made himself master of his whole realm. Still, so long as Darius himself remained at liberty and in the field, no victories could be considered as complete. To capture Darius himself would be the last and crowning act of his conquest. He had now been pursuing him for eighteen hundred miles, advancing slowly from province to province, and from kingdom to kingdom. During all this time the strength of his flying foe had been wasting away. His armies had been broken up, his courage and hope had gradually failed, while the animation and hope of the pursuer had been gathering fresh and increasing strength from his successes, and were excited to wild enthusiasm now, as the hour for the final consummation of all his desires seemed to be drawing nigh.

Guides were ordered to be furnished by the inhabitants, to show the detachment the way across the solitary and desert country. The detachment was to consist of horsemen entirely that they might advance with the utmost celerity. To get as efficient a corps as possible, Alexander dismounted five hundred of the cavalry, and gave their horses to five hundred men—officers and others—selected for their strength and courage from among the foot soldiers. All were ambitious of being designated for this service. Besides the honor of being so selected, there was an intense excitement, as usual toward the close of a chase, to arrive at the end.

This body of horsemen were ready to set out in the evening. Alexander took the command, and, following the guides, they trotted off in the direction which the guides indicated. They traveled all night. When the day dawned, they saw, from an elevation to which they had attained, the body of the Persian troops moving at a short distance before them, foot soldiers, chariots, and horsemen pressing on together in great confusion and disorder.

As soon as Bessus and his company found that their pursuers were close upon them, they attempted at first to hurry forward, in the vain hope of still effecting their escape. Darius was in a chariot. They urged this chariot on, but it moved heavily. Then they concluded to abandon it, and they called upon Darius to mount a horse and ride off with them, leaving the rest of the army and the baggage to its fate. But Darius refused. He said he would rather trust himself in the hands of Alexander than in those of such traitors as they. Rendered desperate by their situation, and exasperated by this reply, Bessus and his confederates thrust their spears into Darius's body, as he sat in his chariot, and then galloped away. They divided into different parties, each taking a different road. Their object in doing this was to increase their chances of escape by confusing Alexander in his plans for pursuing them. Alexander pressed on toward the ground which the enemy were abandoning, and sent off separate detachments after the various divisions of the flying army.

In the mean time Darius remained in his chariot wounded and bleeding. He was worn out and exhausted, both in body and mind, by his complicated sufferings and sorrows. His kingdom lost; his family in captivity; his beloved wife in the grave, where the sorrows and sufferings of separation from her husband had borne her; his cities sacked; his palaces and treasures plundered; and now he himself, in the last hour of his extremity, abandoned and betrayed by all in whom he had placed his confidence and trust, his heart sunk within him in despair. At such a time the soul turns from traitorous friends to an open foe with something like a feeling of confidence and attachment. Darius's exasperation against Bessus was so intense, that his hostility to Alexander became a species of friendship in comparison. He felt that Alexander was a sovereign like himself, and would have some sympathy and fellow-feeling for a sovereign's misfortunes. He thought, too, of his mother, his wife, and his children, and the kindness with which Alexander had treated them went to his heart. He lay there, accordingly, faint and bleeding in his chariot, and looking for the coming of Alexander as for that of a protector and friend, the only one to whom he could now look for any relief in the extremity of his distress.

The Macedonians searched about in various places, thinking it possible that in the sudden dispersion of the enemy Darius might have been left behind. At last the chariot in which he was lying was found. Darius was in it, pierced with spears. The floor of the chariot was covered with blood. They raised him a little, and he spoke. He called for water.

Men wounded and dying on the field of battle are tormented always with an insatiable and intolerable thirst, the manifestations of which constitute one of the greatest horrors of the scene. They cry piteously to all who pass to bring them water, or else to kill them. They crawl along the ground to get at the canteens of their dead companions, in hopes to find, remaining in them, some drops to drink; and if there is a little brook meandering through the battle-field, its bed gets filled and choked up with the bodies of those who crawled there, in their agony, to quench their horrible thirst, and die. Darius was suffering this thirst. It bore down and silenced, for the time, every other suffering, so that his first cry, when his enemies came around him with shouts of exultation, was not for his life, not for mercy, not for relief from the pain and anguish of his wounds—he begged them to give him some water.

He spoke through an interpreter. The interpreter was a Persian prisoner whom the Macedonian army had taken some time before, and who had learned the Greek language in the Macedonian camp. Anticipating some occasion for his services, they had brought him with them now, and it was through him that Darius called for water. A Macedonian soldier went immediately to get some. Others hurried away in search of Alexander, to bring him to the spot where the great object of his hostility, and of his long and protracted pursuit, was dying.

Darius received the drink. He then said that he was extremely glad that they had an interpreter with them, who could understand him, and bear his message to Alexander. He had been afraid that he should have had to die without being able to communicate what he had to say. "Tell Alexander," said he, then, "that I feel under the strongest obligations to him, which I can now never repay, for his kindness to my wife, my mother, and my children. He not only spared their lives, but treated them with the greatest consideration and care, and did all in his power to make them happy. The last feeling in my heart is gratitude to him for these favors. I hope now that he will go on prosperously, and finish his conquests as triumphantly as he has begun them." He would have made one last request, he added, if he had thought it necessary, and that was, that Alexander would pursue the traitor Bessus, and avenge the murder he had committed; but he was sure that Alexander would do this of his own accord, as the punishment of such treachery was an object of common interest for every king.

Darius then took Polystratus, the Macedonian who had brought him the water, by the hand, saying, "Give Alexander thy hand as I now give thee mine; it is the pledge of my gratitude and affection."

Darius was too weak to say much more. They gathered around him, endeavoring to sustain his strength until Alexander should arrive; but it was all in vain. He sank gradually, and soon ceased to breathe. Alexander came up a few minutes after all was over. He was at first shocked at the spectacle before him, and then overwhelmed with grief. He wept bitterly. Some compunctions of conscience may have visited his heart at seeing thus before him the ruin he had made. Darius had never injured him or done him any wrong, and yet here he lay, hunted to death by a persevering and relentless hostility, for which his conqueror had no excuse but his innate love of dominion over his fellow-men. Alexander spread his own military cloak over the dead body. He immediately made arrangements for having the body embalmed, and then sent it to Susa, for Sysigambis, in a very costly coffin, and with a procession of royal magnificence. He sent it to her that she might have the satisfaction of seeing it deposited in the tombs of the Persian kings. What a present! The killer of a son sending the dead body, in a splendid coffin, to the mother, as a token of respectful regard!

Alexander pressed on to the northward and eastward in pursuit of Bessus, who had soon collected the scattered remains of his army, and was doing his utmost to get into a posture of defense. He did not, however, overtake him till he had crossed the Oxus, a large river which will be found upon the map, flowing to the northward and westward into the Caspian Sea. He had great difficulty in crossing this river, as it was too deep to be forded, and the banks and bottom were so sandy and yielding that he could not make the foundations of bridges stand. He accordingly made floats and rafts, which were supported by skins made buoyant by inflation, or by being stuffed with straw and hay. After getting his army, which had been in the mean time greatly re-enforced and strengthened, across this river, he moved on. The generals under Bessus, finding all hope of escape failing them, resolved on betraying him as he had betrayed his commander. They sent word to Alexander that if he would send forward a small force where they should indicate, they would give up Bessus to his hands. Alexander did so, intrusting the command to an officer named Ptolemy. Ptolemy found Bessus in a small walled town whither he had fled for refuge, and easily took him prisoner. He sent back word to Alexander that Bessus was at his disposal, and asked for orders. The answer was, "Put a rope around his neck and send him to me."

When the wretched prisoner was brought into Alexander's presence, Alexander demanded of him how he could have been so base as to have seized, bound, and at last murdered his kinsman and benefactor. It is a curious instance in proof of the permanence and stability of the great characteristics of human nature, through all the changes of civilization and lapses of time, that Bessus gave the same answer that wrong-doers almost always give when brought to account for their wrongs. He laid the fault upon his accomplices and friends. It was not his act, it was theirs.

Alexander ordered him to be publicly scourged; then he caused his face to be mutilated in a manner customary in those days, when a tyrant wished to stamp upon his victim a perpetual mark of infamy. In this condition, and with a mind in an agony of suspense and fear at the thought of worse tortures which he knew were to come, Alexander sent him as a second present to Sysigambis, to be dealt with, at Susa, as her revenge might direct. She inflicted upon him the most extreme tortures, and finally, when satiated with the pleasure of seeing him suffer, the story is that they chose four very elastic trees, growing at a little distance from each other, and bent down the tops of them toward the central point between them. They fastened the exhausted and dying Bessus to these trees, one limb of his body to each, and then releasing the stems from their confinement, they flew upward, tearing the body asunder, each holding its own dissevered portion, as if in triumph, far over the heads of the multitude assembled to witness the spectacle.

DETERIORATION OF CHARACTER

This state of things was a great cause of mortification and chagrin to the officers of his army. Many of them were older than himself, and better able to resist these temptations to luxury, effeminacy, and vice. They therefore remained firm in their original simplicity and integrity, and after some respectful but ineffectual remonstrances, they stood aloof, alienated from their commander in heart, and condemning very strongly, among themselves, his wickedness and folly.

On the other hand, many of the *younger* officers followed Alexander's example, and became as vain, as irregular, and as fond of vicious indulgence as he. But then, though they joined him in his pleasures, there was no strong bond of union between him and them. The tie which binds mere companions in pleasure together is always very slight and frail. Thus Alexander gradually lost the confidence and affection of his old friends, and gained no new ones. His officers either disapproved his conduct, and were distant and cold, or else joined him in his dissipation and vice, without feeling any real respect for his character, or being bound to him by any principle of fidelity.

Parmenio and his son Philotas were, respectively, striking examples of these two kinds of character. Parmenio was an old general, now considerably advanced in life. He had served, as has already been stated, under Philip, Alexander's father, and had acquired great experience and great fame before Alexander succeeded to the throne. During the whole of Alexander's career Parmenio had been his principal lieutenant general, and he had always placed his greatest reliance upon him in all trying emergencies. He was cool, calm, intrepid, sagacious. He held Alexander back from many rash enterprises, and was the efficient means of his accomplishing most of his plans. It is the custom among all nations to give kings the glory of all that is effected by their generals and officers; and the writers of those days would, of course, in narrating the exploits of the Macedonian army, exaggerate the share which Alexander had in their performances, and underrate those of Parmenio. But in modern times, many impartial readers, in reviewing calmly these events, think that there is reason to doubt whether Alexander, if he had set out on his great expedition without Parmenio, would have succeeded at all.

Philotas was the son of Parmenio, but he was of a very different character. The difference was one which is very often, in all ages of the world, to be observed between those who *inherit* greatness and those who acquire it for themselves. We see the same analogy reigning at the present day, when the sons of the wealthy, who are *born* to fortune, substitute pride, and arrogance, and vicious self-indulgence and waste for the modesty, and prudence, and virtue of their sires, by means of which the fortune was acquired. Philotas was proud, boastful, extravagant, and addicted, like Alexander his master, to every species of indulgence and dissipation. He was universally hated. His father, out of patience with his haughty airs, his boastings, and his pomp and parade, advised him, one day, to "make himself less." But Parmenio's prudent advice to his son was thrown away. Philotas spoke of himself as Alexander's great reliance. "What would Philip have been or have done," said he, "without my father Parmenio? and what would Alexander have been, or have done, without me?" These things were reported to Alexander, and thus the mind of each was filled with suspicion, fear, and hatred toward the other.

Courts and camps are always the scenes of conspiracy and treason, and Alexander was continually hearing of conspiracies and plots formed against him. The strong sentiment of love and devotion with which he inspired all around him at the commencement of his career, was now gone, and his generals and officers were continually planning schemes to depose him from the power which he seemed no longer to have the energy to wield; or, at least, Alexander was continually suspecting that such plans were formed, and he was kept in a continual state of uneasiness and anxiety in discovering and punishing them.

At last a conspiracy occurred in which Philotas was implicated. Alexander was informed one day that a plot had been formed to depose and destroy him; that Philotas had been made acquainted with it by a friend of Alexander's in order that he might make it known to the king; that he had neglected to do so, thus making it probable that he was himself in league with the conspirators. Alexander was informed that the leader and originator of this conspiracy was one of his generals named Dymnus.

He immediately sent an officer to Dymnus to summon him into his presence. Dymnus appeared to be struck with consternation at this summons. Instead of obeying it, he drew his sword, thrust it into his own heart, and fell dead upon the ground.

Alexander then sent for Philotas, and asked him if it was indeed true that he had been informed of this conspiracy, and had neglected to make it known.

Philotas replied that he had been told that such a plot was formed, but that he did not believe it; that such stories were continually invented by the malice of evil-disposed men, and that he had not considered the report which came to his ears as worthy of any attention. He was, however, now convinced, by the terror which Dymnus had manifested, and by his suicide, that all was true, and he asked Alexander's pardon for not having taken immediate measures for communicating promptly the information he had received.

Alexander gave him his hand, said that he was convinced that he was innocent, and had acted as he did from disbelief in the existence of the conspiracy, and not from any guilty participation in it. So Philotas went away to his tent.

Alexander, however, did not drop the subject here. He called a council of his ablest and best friends and advisers, consisting of the principal officers of his army, and laid the facts before them. They came to a different conclusion from his in respect to the guilt of Philotas. They believed him implicated in the crime, and demanded his trial. Trial in such a case, in those days, meant putting the accused to the torture, with a view of forcing him to confess his guilt.

Alexander yielded to this proposal. Perhaps he had secretly instigated it. The advisers of kings and conquerors, in such circumstances as this, generally have the sagacity to discover what advice will be agreeable. At all events, Alexander followed the advice of his counselors, and made arrangements for arresting Philotas on that very evening.

These circumstances occurred at a time when the army was preparing for a march, the various generals lodging in tents pitched for the purpose. Alexander placed extra guards in various parts of the encampment, as if to impress the whole army with a sense of the importance and solemnity of the occasion. He then sent officers to the tent of Philotas, late at night, to arrest him. The officers found their unhappy victim asleep. They awoke him, and made known their errand. Philotas arose, and obeyed the summons, dejected and distressed, aware, apparently, that his destruction was impending.

The next morning Alexander called together a large assembly, consisting of the principal and most important portions of the army, to the number of several thousands. They came together with an air of impressive solemnity, expecting, from the preliminary preparations, that business of very solemn moment was to come before them, though they knew not what it was.

These impressions of awe and solemnity were very much increased by the spectacle which first met the eyes of the assembly after they were convened. This spectacle was that of the dead body of Dymnus, bloody and ghastly, which Alexander ordered to be brought in and exposed to view. The death of Dymnus had been kept a secret, so that the appearance of his body was an unexpected as well as a shocking sight. When the first feeling of surprise and wonder had a little subsided, Alexander explained to the assembly the nature of the conspiracy, and the circumstances connected with the self-execution of one of the guilty participators in it. The spectacle of the body, and the statement of the king, produced a scene of great and universal excitement in the assembly, and this excitement was raised to the highest pitch by the announcement which Alexander now made, that he had reason to believe that Philotas and his father Parmenio, officers who had enjoyed his highest favor, and in whom he had placed the most unbounded confidence, were the authors and originators of the whole design.

He then ordered Philotas to be brought in. He came guarded as a criminal, with his hands tied behind him, and his head covered with a coarse cloth. He was in a state of great dejection and despondency. It is true that he was brought forward for trial, but he knew very well that trial meant torture, and that there was no hope for him as to the result. Alexander said that he would leave the accused to be dealt with by the assembly, and withdrew.

The authorities of the army, who now had the proud and domineering spirit which had so long excited their hatred and envy completely in their power, listened for a time to what Philotas had to say in his own justification. He showed that there was no evidence whatever against him, and appealed to their sense of justice not to condemn him on mere vague surmises. In reply, they decided to put him to the torture. There was no evidence, it was true, and they wished, accordingly, to supply its place by his own confession, extorted by pain. Of course, his most inveterate and implacable enemies were appointed to conduct the operation. They put Philotas upon the rack. The rack is an instrument of wheels and pulleys, into which the victim is placed, and his limbs and tendons are stretched by it in a manner which produces most excruciating pain.

Philotas bore the beginning of his torture with great resolution and fortitude. He made no complaint, he uttered no cry: this was the signal to his executioners to increase the tension and the agony. Of course, in such a trial as this, there was no question of guilt or innocence at issue. The only question was, which could stand out the longest, his enemies in witnessing horrible sufferings, or he himself in enduring them. In this contest the unhappy Philotas was vanquished at last. He begged them to release him from the rack, saying he would confess whatever they required, on condition of being allowed to die in peace.

They accordingly released him, and, in answer to their questions, he confessed that he himself and his father were involved in the plot. He said yes to various other inquiries relating to the circumstances of the conspiracy, and to the guilt of various individuals whom those that managed the torture had suspected, or who, at any rate, they wished to have condemned. The answers of Philotas to all these questions were written down, and he was himself sentenced to be stoned. The sentence was put in execution without any delay.

During all this time Parmenio was in Media, in command of a very important part of Alexander's army. It was decreed that he must die; but some careful management was necessary to secure his execution while he was at so great a distance, and at the head of so great a force. The affair had to be conducted with great secrecy as well as dispatch. The plan adopted was as follows:

There was a certain man, named Polydamas, who was regarded as Parmenio's particular friend. Polydamas was commissioned to go to Media and see the execution performed. He was selected, because it was supposed that if any enemy, or a stranger, had been sent, Parmenio would have received him with suspicion, or at least with caution, and kept himself on his guard. They gave Polydamas several letters to Parmenio, as if from his friends, and to one of them they attached the seal of his son Philotas, the more completely to deceive the unhappy father. Polydamas was eleven days on his journey into Media. He had letters to Cleander, the governor of the province of Media, which contained the king's warrant for Parmenio's execution. He arrived at the house of Cleander in the night. He delivered his letters, and they together concerted the plans for carrying the execution into effect.

After having taken all the precautions necessary, Polydamas went, with many attendants accompanying him, to the quarters of Parmenio. The old general, for he was at this time eighty years of age, was walking in his grounds. Polydamas being admitted, ran up to accost him, with great appearance of cordiality and friendship. He delivered to him his letters, and Parmenio read them. He seemed much pleased with their contents, especially with the one which had been written in the name of his son. He had no means of detecting the imposture, for it was very customary in those days for letters to be written by secretaries, and to be authenticated solely by the seal.

Parmenio was much pleased to get good tidings from Alexander, and from his son, and began conversing upon the contents of the letters, when Polydamas, watching his opportunity, drew forth a dagger which he had concealed upon his person, and plunged it into Parmenio's side. He drew it forth immediately and struck it at his throat. The attendants rushed on at this signal, and thrust their swords again and again into the fallen body until it ceased to breathe.

The death of Parmenio and of his son in this violent manner, when, too, there was so little evidence of their guilt, made a very general and a very unfavorable impression in respect to Alexander; and not long afterward another case occurred, in some respects still more painful, as it evinced still more strikingly that the mind of Alexander, which had been in his earlier days filled with such noble and lofty sentiments of justice and generosity, was gradually getting to be under the supreme dominion of selfish and ungovernable passions: it was the case of Clitus.

Clitus was a very celebrated general of Alexander's army, and a great favorite with the king. He had, in fact, on one occasion saved Alexander's life. It was at the battle of the Granicus. Alexander had exposed himself in the thickest of the combat, and was surrounded by enemies. The sword of one of them was actually raised over his head, and would have fallen and killed him on the spot, if Clitus had not rushed forward and cut the man down just at the instant when he was about striking the blow. Such acts of fidelity and courage as this had given Alexander great confidence in Clitus. It happened, shortly after the death of Parmenio, that the governor of one of the most important provinces of the empire resigned his post. Alexander appointed Clitus to fill the vacancy.

The evening before his departure to take charge of his government, Alexander invited him to a banquet, made, partly at least, in honor of his elevation. Clitus and the other guests assembled. They drank wine, as usual, with great freedom. Alexander became excited, and began to speak, as he was now often accustomed to do, boastingly of his own exploits, and to disparage those of his father Philip in comparison.

Men half intoxicated are very prone to quarrel, and not the less so for being excellent friends when sober. Clitus had served under Philip. He was now an old man, and, like other old men, was very tenacious of the glory that belonged to the exploits of his youth. He was very restless and uneasy at hearing Alexander claim for himself the merit of his father Philip's victory at Chæronea, and began to murmur something to those who sat next to him about kings claiming and getting a great deal of glory which did not belong to them.

Alexander asked what it was that Clitus said. No one replied. Clitus, however, went on talking, speaking more and more audibly as he became gradually more and more excited. He praised the character of Philip, and applauded his military exploits, saying that they were far superior to any of the enterprises of *their* day. The different parties at the table took up the subject, and began to dispute, the old men taking the part of Philip and former days, and the younger defending Alexander. Clitus became more and more excited. He praised Parmenio, who had been Philip's greatest general, and began to impugn the justice of his late condemnation and death.

Alexander retorted, and Clitus, rising from his seat, and losing now all self-command, reproached him with severe and bitter words. "Here is the hand," said he, extending his arm, "that saved your life at the battle of the Granicus, and the fate of Parmenio shows what sort of gratitude and what rewards faithful servants are to expect at your hands." Alexander, burning with rage, commanded Clitus to leave the table. Clitus obeyed, saying, as he moved away, "He is right not to bear freeborn men at his table who can only tell him the truth. He is right. It is fitting for him to pass his life among barbarians and slaves, who will be proud to pay their adoration to his Persian girdle and his splendid robe."

Alexander seized a javelin to hurl at Clitus's head. The guests rose in confusion, and with many outcries pressed around him. Some seized Alexander's arm, some began to hurry Clitus out of the room, and some were engaged in loudly criminating and threatening each other. They got Clitus out of the apartment, but as soon as he was in the hall he broke away from them, returned by another door, and began to renew his insults to Alexander. The king hurled his javelin and struck Clitus down, saying, at the same time, "Go, then, and join Philip and

Parmenio." The company rushed to the rescue of the unhappy man, but it was too late. He died almost immediately.

Alexander, as soon as he came to himself, was overwhelmed with remorse and despair. He mourned bitterly, for many days, the death of his long-tried and faithful friend, and execrated the intoxication and passion, on his part, which had caused it. He could not, however, restore Clitus to life, nor remove from his own character the indelible stains which such deeds necessarily fixed upon it.

ALEXANDER'S END

AFTER the events narrated in the last chapter, Alexander continued, for two or three years, his expeditions and conquests in Asia, and in the course of them he met with a great variety of adventures which can not be here particularly described. He penetrated into India as far as the banks of the Indus, and, not content with this, was preparing to cross the Indus and go on to the Ganges. His soldiers, however, resisted this design. They were alarmed at the stories which they heard of the Indian armies, with elephants bearing castles upon their backs, and soldiers armed with strange and unheard-of weapons. These rumors, and the natural desire of the soldiers not to go away any further from their native land, produced almost a mutiny in the army. At length, Alexander, learning how strong and how extensive the spirit of insubordination was becoming, summoned his officers to his own tent, and then ordering the whole army to gather around, he went out to meet them.

He made an address to them, in which he recounted all their past exploits, praised the courage and perseverance which they had shown thus far, and endeavored to animate them with a desire to proceed. They listened in silence, and no one attempted to reply. This solemn pause was followed by marks of great agitation throughout the assembly. The army loved their commander, notwithstanding his faults and failings. They were extremely unwilling to make any resistance to his authority; but they had lost that extreme and unbounded confidence in his energy and virtue which made them ready, in the former part of his career, to press forward into any difficulties and dangers whatever, where he led the way.

At last one of the army approached the king and addressed him somewhat as follows:

"We are not changed, sir, in our affection for you. We still have, and shall always retain, the same zeal and the same fidelity. We are ready to follow you at the hazard of our lives, and to march wherever you may lead us. Still we must ask you, most respectfully, to consider the circumstances in which we are placed. We have done all for you that it was possible for man to do. We have crossed seas and land. We have marched to the end of the world, and you are now meditating the conquest of another, by going in search of new Indias, unknown to the Indians themselves. Such a thought may be worthy of your courage and resolution, but it surpasses ours, and our strength still more. Look at these ghastly faces, and these bodies covered with wounds and scars. Remember how numerous we were when first we set out with you, and see how few of us remain. The few who have escaped so many toils and dangers have neither courage nor strength to follow you any further. They all long to revisit their country and their homes, and to enjoy, for the remainder of their lives, the fruits of all their toils. Forgive them these desires, so natural to man."

The expression of these sentiments confirmed and strengthened them in the minds of all the soldiers. Alexander was greatly troubled and distressed. A disaffection in a small part of an army may be put down by decisive measures; but when the determination to resist is universal, it is useless for any commander, however imperious and absolute in temper, to attempt to withstand it. Alexander, however, was extremely unwilling to yield. He remained two days shut up in his tent, the prey to disappointment and chagrin.

The result, however, was, that he abandoned plans of further conquest, and turned his steps again toward the west. He met with various adventures as he went on, and incurred many dangers, often in a rash and foolish manner, and for no good end. At one time, while attacking a small town, he seized a scaling ladder and mounted with the troops. In doing this, however, he put himself forward so rashly and inconsiderately that his ladder was broken, and while the rest retreated he was left alone upon the wall, whence he descended into the town, and was immediately surrounded by enemies. His friends raised their ladders again, and pressed on desperately to find and rescue him. Some gathered around him and defended him, while others contrived to open a small gate, by which the rest of the army gained admission. By this means Alexander was saved; though, when they brought him out of the city, there was an arrow three feet long, which could not be extracted, sticking into his side through his coat of mail.

The surgeons first very carefully out off the wooden shaft of the arrow, and then, enlarging the wound by incisions, they drew out the barbed point. The soldiers were indignant that Alexander should expose his person in such a fool hardy way, only to endanger himself, and to compel them to rush into danger to rescue him The wound very nearly proved fatal. The loss of blood was attended with extreme exhaustion; still, in the course of a few weeks he recovered.

Alexander's habits of intoxication and vicious excess of all kinds were, in the mean time, continually increasing. He not only indulged in such excesses himself, but he encouraged them in others. He would offer prizes at his banquets to those who would drink the most. On one of these occasions, the man who conquered drank, it is said, eighteen or twenty pints of wine, after which he lingered in misery for three days, and then died; and more than forty others, present at the same entertainment, died in consequence of their excesses.

Alexander returned toward Babylon. His friend Hephæstion was with him, sharing with him every where in all the vicious indulgences to which he had become so prone. Alexander gradually separated himself more and more from his old Macedonian friends, and linked himself more and more closely with Persian associates. He married Statira, the oldest daughter of Darius, and gave the youngest daughter to Hephæstion. He encouraged similar marriages between Macedonian officers and Persian maidens, as far as he could. In a word, he seemed intent in merging, in every way, his original character and habits of action in the effeminacy, luxury, and vice of the Eastern world, which he had at first so looked down upon and despised.

Alexander's entrance into Babylon, on his return from his Indian campaigns, was a scene of great magnificence and splendor. Embassadors and princes had assembled there from almost all the nations of the earth to receive and welcome him, and the most ample preparations were made for processions, shows, parades, and spectacles to do him honor. The whole country was in a state of extreme excitement, and the most expensive preparations were made to give him a reception worthy of one who was the conqueror and monarch of the world, and the son of a god.

When Alexander approached the city, however, he was met by a deputation of Chaldean astrologers. The astrologers were a class of philosophers who pretended, in those days, to foretell human events by means of the motions of the stars. The motions of the stars were studied very closely in early times, and in those Eastern countries, by the shepherds, who had often to remain in the open air, through the summer nights, to watch their flocks. These shepherds observed that nearly all the stars were *fixed* in relation to each other, that is, although they rose successively in the east, and, passing over, set in the west, they did not change in relation to each other. There were, however, a few that wandered about among the rest in an irregular and unaccountable manner. They called these stars the wanderers—that is, in their language, *the planets*—and they watched their mysterious movements with great interest and awe. They naturally imagined that these changes had some connection with human affairs, and they endeavored to prognosticate from them the events, whether prosperous or adverse, which were to befall mankind. Whenever a comet or an eclipse appeared, they thought it portended some terrible calamity. The study of the motions and appearances of the stars, with a view to foretell the course of human affairs, was the science of astrology.

The astrologers came, in a very solemn and imposing procession, to meet Alexander on his march. They informed him that they had found indubitable evidence in the stars that, if he came into Babylon, he would hazard his life. They accordingly begged him not to approach any nearer, but to choose some other city for his capital. Alexander was very much perplexed by this announcement. His mind, weakened by effeminacy and dissipation, was very susceptible to superstitious fears. It was not merely by the debilitating influence of vicious indulgence on the nervous constitution that this effect was produced. It was, in part, the moral influence of conscious guilt. Guilt makes men afraid. It not only increases the power of real dangers, but predisposes the mind to all sorts of imaginary fears.

Alexander was very much troubled at this announcement of the astrologers. He suspended his march, and began anxiously to consider what to do. At length the Greek philosophers came to him and reasoned with him on the subject, persuading him that the science of astrology was not worthy of any belief. The Greeks had no faith in astrology. They foretold future events by the flight of birds, or by the appearances presented in the dissection of beasts offered in sacrifice!

At length, however, Alexander's fears were so far allayed that he concluded to enter the city. He advanced, accordingly, with his whole army, and made his entry under circumstances of the greatest possible parade and splendor. As soon, however, as the excitement of the first few days had passed away, his mind relapsed again, and he became anxious, troubled, and unhappy.

Hephæstion, his great personal friend and companion, had died while he was on the march toward Babylon. He was brought to the grave by diseases produced by dissipation and vice. Alexander was very much moved by his death. It threw him at once into a fit of despondency and gloom. It was some time before he could at all overovercome the melancholy reflections and forebodings which this event produced. He determined that, as soon as he arrived in Babylon, he would do all possible honor to Hephæstion's memory by a magnificent funeral.

He accordingly now sent orders to all the cities and kingdoms around, and collected a vast sum for this purpose. He had a part of the city wall pulled down to furnish a site for a monumental edifice. This edifice was constructed of an enormous size and most elaborate architecture. It was ornamented with long rows of prows of ships, taken by Alexander in his victories, and by statues, and columns, and sculptures, and gilded ornaments of every kind. There were images of sirens on the entablatures near the roof, which, by means of a mechanism concealed within, were made to sing dirges and mournful songs. The expense of this edifice, and of the games, shows, and spectacles connected with its consecration, is said by the historians of the day to have been a sum which, on calculation, is found equal to about ten millions of dollars.

There were, however, some limits still to Alexander's extravagance and folly. There was a mountain in Greece, Mount Athos, which a certain projector said could be carved and fashioned into the form of a man—probably in a recumbent posture. There was a city on one of the declivities of the mountain, and a small river, issuing from springs in the ground, came down on the other side. The artist who conceived of this prodigious piece of sculpture said that he would so shape the figure that the city should be in one of its hands, and the river should flow out from the other.

Alexander listened to this proposal. The name Mount Athos recalled to his mind the attempt of Xerxes, a former Persian king, who had attempted to cut a road through the rocks upon a part of Mount Athos, in the invasion of Greece. He did not succeed, but left the unfinished work a lasting memorial both of the attempt and the failure. Alexander concluded at length that he would not attempt such a sculpture. "Mount Athos," said he, "is already the monument of one king's folly; I will not make it that of another."

As soon as the excitement connected with the funeral obsequies of Hephæstion were over, Alexander's mind relapsed again into a state of gloomy melancholy. This depression, caused, as it was, by previous dissipation and vice, seemed to admit of no remedy or relief but in new excesses. The traces, however, of his former energy so far remained that he began to form magnificent plans for the improvement of Babylon. He commenced the execution of some of these plans. His time was spent, in short, in strange alternations: resolution and energy in forming vast plans one day, and utter abandonment to all the excesses of dissipation and vice the next. It was a mournful spectacle to see his former greatness of soul still struggling on, though more and more faintly, as it became gradually overborne by the resistless inroads of intemperance and sin. The scene was at length suddenly terminated in the following manner:

PROPOSED IMPROVEMENT OF MOUNT ATHOS

On one occasion, after he had spent a whole night in drinking and carousing, the guests, when the usual time arrived for separating, proposed that, instead of this, they should begin anew, and commence a second banquet at the end of the first. Alexander, half intoxicated already, entered warmly into this proposal. They assembled, accordingly, in a very short time. There were twenty present at this new feast. Alexander, to show how far he was from having exhausted his powers of drinking, began to pledge each one of the company individually. Then he drank to them all together. There was a very large cup, called the bowl of Hercules, which he now called for, and, after having filled it to the brim, he drank it off to the health of one of the company present, a Macedonian named Proteas. This feat being received by the company with great applause, he ordered the great bowl to be filled again, and drank it off as before.

The work was now done. His faculties and his strength soon failed him, and he sank down to the floor. They bore him away to his palace. A violent fever intervened, which the physicians did all in their power to allay. As soon as his reason returned a little, Alexander aroused himself from his lethargy, and tried to persuade himself that he should recover. He began to issue orders in regard to the army, and to his ships, as if such a turning of his mind to the thoughts of power and empire would help bring him back from the brink of the grave toward which he had been so obviously tending. He was determined, in fact, that he would not die.

He soon found, however, notwithstanding his efforts to be vigorous and resolute, that his strength was fast ebbing away. The vital powers had received a fatal wound, and he soon felt that they could sustain themselves but little longer. He came to the conclusion that he must die. He drew his signet ring off from his finger; it was a token that he felt that all was over. He handed the ring to one of his friends who stood by his bed-side. "When I am gone," said he, "take my body to the Temple of Jupiter Ammon, and inter it there."

The generals who were around him advanced to his bed-side, and one after another kissed his hand. Their old affection for him revived as they saw him about to take leave of them forever. They asked him to whom he wished to leave his empire. "To the most worthy," said he. He meant, doubtless, by this evasion, that he was too weak and exhausted to think of such affairs. He knew, probably, that it was useless for him to attempt to control the government of his empire after his death. He said, in fact, that he foresaw that the decision of such questions would give rise to some strange funeral games after his decease. Soon after this he died.

The palaces of Babylon were immediately filled with cries of mourning at the death of the prince, followed by bitter and interminable disputes about the succession. It had not been the aim of Alexander's life to establish firm and well-settled governments in the countries that he conquered, to encourage order, and peace, and industry among men, and to introduce system and regularity in human affairs, so as to leave the world in a better condition than he found it. In this respect his course of conduct presents a strong contrast with that of Washington. It was Washington's aim to mature and perfect organizations which would move on prosperously of themselves, without him; and he was continually withdrawing his hand from action and control in public affairs, taking a higher pleasure in the independent working of the institutions which he had formed and protected, than in exercising, himself, a high personal power. Alexander, on the other hand, was all his life intent solely on enlarging and strengthening his own personal power. *He* was all in all. He wished to make himself so. He never thought of the welfare of the countries which he had subjected to his sway, or did any thing to guard against the anarchy and civil wars which he knew full well would break out at once over all his vast dominions, as soon as his power came to an end.

The result was as might have been foreseen. The whole vast field of his conquests became, for many long and weary years after Alexander's death, the prey to the most ferocious and protracted civil wars. Each general and governor seized the power which Alexander's death left in his hands, and endeavored to defend himself in the possession of it against the others. Thus the devastation and misery which the making of these conquests brought upon Europe and Asia were continued for many years during the slow and terrible process of their return to their original condition.

In the exigency of the moment, however, at Alexander's death, the generals who were in his court at the time assembled forthwith, and made an attempt to appoint some one to take the immediate command. They spent a week in stormy debates on this subject. Alexander had left no legitimate heir, and he had declined when on his death-bed, as we have already seen, to appoint a successor. Among his wives—if, indeed, they may be called wives—there was one named Roxana, who had a son not long after his death. This son was ultimately named his successor; but, in the mean time, a certain relative named Aridæus was chosen by the generals to assume the command. The selection of Aridæus was a sort of compromise. He had no talents or capacity whatever, and was chosen by the rest on that very account, each one thinking that if such an imbecile as Aridæus was nominally the king, he could himself manage to get possession of the real power. Aridæus accepted the appointment, but he was never able to make himself king in any thing but the name.

In the mean time, as the tidings of Alexander's death spread over the empire, it produced very various effects, according to the personal feelings in respect to Alexander entertained by the various personages and powers to which the intelligence came. Some, who had admired his greatness, and the splendor of his exploits, without having themselves experienced the bitter fruits of them, mourned and lamented his death. Others, whose fortunes had been ruined, and whose friends and relatives had been destroyed, in the course, or in the sequel of his victories, rejoiced that he who had been such a scourge and curse to others, had himself sunk, at last under the just judgment of Heaven.

We should have expected that Sysigambis, the bereaved and widowed mother of Darius, would have been among those who would have exulted most highly at the conqueror's death; but history tells us that, instead of this, she mourned over it with a protracted and inconsolable grief. Alexander had been, in fact, though the implacable enemy of her son, a faithful and generous friend to her. He had treated her, at all times, with the utmost respect and consideration, had supplied all her wants, and ministered, in every way, to her comfort and happiness. She had gradually learned to think of him and to love him as a son; he, in fact, always called her mother; and when she learned that he was gone, she felt as if her last earthly protector was gone. Her life had been one continued scene of affliction and sorrow, and this last blow brought her to her end. She pined away, perpetually restless and distressed. She lost all desire for food, and refused, like others who are suffering great mental anguish, to take the sustenance which her friends and attendants offered and urged upon her. At length she died. They said she starved herself to death; but it was, probably, grief and despair at being thus left, in her declining years, so hopelessly friendless and alone, and not hunger, that destroyed her.

In striking contrast to this mournful scene of sorrow in the palace of Sysigambis, there was an exhibition of the most wild and tumultuous joy in the streets, and in all the public places of resort in the city of Athens, when the tidings of the death of the great Macedonian king arrived there. The Athenian commonwealth, as well as all the other states of Southern Greece, had submitted very reluctantly to the Macedonian supremacy. They had resisted Philip, and they had resisted Alexander. Their opposition had been at last suppressed and silenced by Alexander's terrible vengeance upon Thebes, but it never was really subdued. Demosthenes, the orator, who had exerted so powerful an influence against the Macedonian kings, had been sent into banishment, and all outward expressions of discontent were restrained. The discontent and hostility existed still, however, as inveterate as ever, and was ready to break out anew, with redoubled violence, the moment that the terrible energy of Alexander himself was no longer to be feared.

When, therefore, the rumor arrived at Athens—for at first it was a mere rumor—that Alexander was dead in Babylon, the whole city was thrown into a state of the most tumultuous joy. The citizens assembled in the public places, and congratulated and harangued each other with expressions of the greatest exultation. They were for proclaiming their independence and declaring war against Macedon on the spot. Some of the older and more sagacious of their counselors were, however, more composed and calm. They recommended a little delay, in order to see whether the news was really true. Phocion, in particular, who was one of the prominent statesmen of the city, endeavored to quiet the excitement of the people. "Do not let us be so precipitate," said he. "There is time enough. If Alexander is really dead to-day, he will be dead to-morrow, and the next day, so that there will be time enough for us to act with deliberation and discretion."

Just and true as this view of the subject was, there was too much of rebuke and satire in it to have much influence with those to whom it was addressed. The people were resolved on war. They sent commissioners into all the states of the Peloponnesus to organize a league, offensive and defensive, against Macedon. They recalled Demosthenes from his banishment, and adopted all the necessary military measures for establishing and maintaining their freedom. The consequences of all this would doubtless have been very serious, if the rumor of Alexander's death had proved false; but, fortunately for Demosthenes and the Athenians, it was soon abundantly confirmed.

The return of Demosthenes to the city was like the triumphal entry of a conqueror. At the time of his recall he was at the island of Ægina, which is about forty miles southwest of Athens, in one of the gulfs of the Ægean Sea. They sent a public galley to receive him, and to bring him to the land. It was a galley of three banks of oars, and was fitted up in a style to do honor to a public guest. Athens is situated some distance back from the sea, and has a small port, called the Piræus, at the shore—a long, straight avenue leading from the port to the city. The galley by which Demosthenes was conveyed landed at the Piræus. All the civil and religious authorities of the city went down to the port, in a grand procession, to receive and welcome the exile on his arrival, and a large portion of the population followed in the train, to witness the spectacle, and to swell by their acclamations the general expression of joy.

In the mean time, the preparations for Alexander's funeral had been going on, upon a great scale of magnificence and splendor. It was two years before they were complete. The body had been given, first, to be embalmed, according to the Egyptian and Chaldean art, and then had been placed in a sort of sarcophagus, in which it was to be conveyed to its long home. Alexander, it will be remembered, had given directions that it should be taken to the temple of Jupiter Ammon, in the Egyptian oasis, where he had been pronounced the son of a god. It would seem incredible that such a mind as his could really admit such an absurd superstition as the story of his divine origin, and we must there-therefore suppose that he gave this direction in order that the place of his interment might confirm the idea of his superhuman nature in the general opinion of mankind. At all events, such were his orders, and the authorities who were left in power at Babylon after his death, prepared to execute them.

It was a long journey. To convey a body by a regular funeral procession, formed as soon after the death as the arrangements could be made, from Babylon to the eastern frontiers of Egypt, a distance of a thousand miles, was perhaps as grand a plan of interment as was ever formed. It has something like a parallel in the removal of Napoleon's body from St. Helena to Paris, though this was not really an interment, but a transfer. Alexander's was a simple burial procession, going from the palace where he died to the proper cemetery—a march of a thousand miles, it is true, but all within his own dominions. The greatness of it resulted simply from the magnitude of the scale on which every thing pertaining to the mighty here was performed, for it was nothing but a simple passage from the dwelling to the burial-ground in his own estates, after all.

A very large and elaborately constructed carriage was built to convey the body. The accounts of the richness and splendor of this vehicle are almost incredible. The spokes and naves of the wheels were overlaid with gold, and the extremities of the axles, where they appeared outside at the centers of the wheels, were adorned with massive golden ornaments. The wheels and axle-trees were so large, and so far apart, that there was supported upon them a platform or floor for the carriage twelve feet wide and eighteen feet long. Upon this platform there was erected a magnificent pavilion, supported by Ionic columns, and profusely ornamented, both within and without, with purple and gold. The interior constituted an apartment, more or less open at the sides, and resplendent within with gems and precious stones. The space of twelve feet by eighteen forms a chamber of no inconsiderable size, and there was thus ample room for what was required within. There was a throne, raised some steps, and placed back upon the platform, profusely carved and gilded. It was empty; but crowns, representing the various nations over whom Alexander had reigned, were hung upon it. At the foot of the throne was the coffin, made, it is said, of solid gold, and containing, besides the body, a large quantity of the most costly spices and aromatic perfumes, which filled the air with their odor. The arms which Alexander wore were laid out in view, also, between the coffin and the throne.

On the four sides of the carriage were *bass relievos*, that is, sculptured figures raised from a surface, representing Alexander himself, with various military concomitants. There were Macedonian columns, and Persian squadrons, and elephants of India, and troops of horse, and various other emblems of the departed hero's greatness and power. Around the pavilion, too, there was a fringe or net-work of golden lace, to the pendents of which were attached bells, which tolled continually, with a mournful sound, as the carriage moved along. A long column of mules, sixty-four in number, arranged in sets of four, drew this ponderous car. These mules were all selected for their great size and strength, and were splendidly caparisoned. They had collars and harnesses mounted with gold, and enriched with precious stones.

Before the procession set out from Babylon an army of pioneers and workmen went forward to repair the roads, strengthen the bridges, and remove the obstacles along the whole line of route over which the train was to pass. At length, when all was ready, the solemn procession began to move, and passed out through the gates of Babylon. No pen can describe the enormous throngs of spectators that assembled to witness its departure, and that gathered along the route, as it passed slowly on from city to city, in its long and weary way.

Notwithstanding all this pomp and parade, however, the body never reached its intended destination. Ptolemy, the officer to whom Egypt fell in the division of Alexander's empire, came forth with a grand escort of troops to meet the funeral procession as it came into Egypt. He preferred, for some reason or other, that the body should be interred in the city of Alexandria. It was accordingly deposited there, and a great monument was erected over the spot. This monument is said to have remained standing for fifteen hundred years, but all vestiges of it have now disappeared. The city of Alexandria itself, however, is the conqueror's real monument; the greatest and best, perhaps, that any conqueror ever left behind him. It is a monument, too, that time will not destroy; its position and character, as Alexander foresaw, by bringing it a continued renovation, secure its perpetuity.

Alexander earned well the name and reputation of THE GREAT. He was truly great in all those powers and capacities which can elevate one man above his fellows. We can not help applauding the extraordinary energy of his genius, though we condemn the selfish and cruel ends to which his life was devoted. He was simply a robber, but yet a robber on so vast a scale, that mankind, in contemplating his career, have generally lost sight of the wickedness of his crimes in their admiration of the enormous magnitude of the scale on which they were perpetrated.

Also from Benediction Books …
American History Stories
Volumes I-IV
Mara L. Pratt
Benediction Classics,2011
Each c200 pages
ISBN:
Vol I   978-1-84902-412-9
Vol II   978-1-84902-410-5
Vol III   978-1-84902-409-9
Vol IV   978-1-84902-407-5

Available from www.amazon.com,
www.amazon.co.uk

History is brought to life in these four volumes of Mara L. Pratt's
retelling of the history of America, first published in 1891. The
recommended reading age is 8-12, and the chapters are short with
black and white illustrations, providing a wonderful introduction
for children to American history. They are so compelling that
adults will enjoy them as much as the children.

The first volume begins with the story from Long Ago and ends
with how the colonies great together.

The second volume tells tales of the Revolutionary times, including
the reasons for the American Revolution, the courage of those defending liberty, the early battles and the heroes who led the
colonists to victory.

The third volume covers the period from the end or the Revolutionary War to the middle of the 19th Century. The chapters cover
the Washington and Jefferson administrations, the War of 1812
and some Indian Wars, as well as a series of fascinating well-
known characters of the period.

The final volume covers the period of great conflict from Lincoln
becoming president and the southern states seceding until the end
of the civil war.

Hurlbut's Story of the Bible
Unabridged and fully illustrated in BW
Jesse Lyman Hurlbut
Benediction Classics, 2011
976 pages
Size 11 x 8.5 inches
ISBN: 978-1849024556

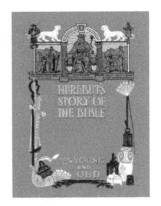

Available from www.amazon.com,
www.amazon.co.uk

In the tradition of parents telling their children stories from the
Bible, this new edition of a delightful book presents a continuous
narrative of the Scriptures that brings the great heroes and events
from the Bible to life. It is unabridged and features 168 stories
from the Old and New Testaments, copious BW illustrations, a
presentation page and a retouched version of the 1904 cover.
Since it was written in 1904 by an American Methodist Episcopal
Clergyman, Jesse Lyman Hurlbut, over 4 million copies have been
distributed.

The Adventures of Sajo and her Beaver People
Grey Owl
Benediction Classics, 2011
164 pages
ISBN: 978-1849024655

Available from www.amazon.com,
www.amazon.co.uk

Grey Owl's children's story, first published in 1935. This delightful novel
comes complete with Grey Owl's orig-
inal drawings, chapter head-pieces and a glossary of Ojibway Indian words.

Also from Benediction Books …
Wandering Between Two Worlds: Essays on Faith and Art
Anita Mathias
Benediction Books, 2007
152 pages
ISBN: 0955373700

Available from www.amazon.com, www.amazon.co.uk

In these wide-ranging lyrical essays, Anita Mathias writes, in lush, lovely prose, of her naughty Catholic childhood in Jamshedpur, India; her large, eccentric family in Mangalore, a sea-coast town converted by the Portuguese in the sixteenth century; her rebellion and atheism as a teenager in her Himalayan boarding school, run by German missionary nuns, St. Mary's Convent, Nainital; and her abrupt religious conversion after which she entered Mother Teresa's convent in Calcutta as a novice. Later rich, elegant essays explore the dualities of her life as a writer, mother, and Christian in the United States-- Domesticity and Art, Writing and Prayer, and the experience of being "an alien and stranger" as an immigrant in America, sensing the need for roots.

About the Author

Anita Mathias is the author of *Wandering Between Two Worlds: Essays on Faith and Art.* She has a B.A. and M.A. in English from Somerville College, Oxford University, and an M.A. in Creative Writing from the Ohio State University, USA. Anita won a National Endowment of the Arts fellowship in Creative Nonfiction in 1997. She lives in Oxford, England with her husband, Roy, and her daughters, Zoe and Irene.

Anita's website:
    http://www.anitamathias.com, and
Anita's blog Dreaming Beneath the Spires:
    http://dreamingbeneaththespires.blogspot.com

The Church That Had Too Much
Anita Mathias
Benediction Books, 2010
52 pages
ISBN: 9781849026567

Available from www.amazon.com, www.amazon.co.uk

The Church That Had Too Much was very well-intentioned. She
wanted to love God, she wanted to love people, but she was both ham-
pered by her muchness and the abundance of her possessions, and
beset by ambition, power struggles and snobbery. Read about the surprising way The Church That Had Too Much began to resolve her
problems in this deceptively simple and enchanting fable.

About the Author

Anita Mathias is the author of *Wandering Between Two Worlds: Essays on Faith and Art*. She has a B.A. and M.A. in English from
Somerville College, Oxford University, and an M.A. in Creative Writing from the Ohio State University, USA. Anita won a National
Endowment of the Arts fellowship in Creative Nonfiction in 1997.
She lives in Oxford, England with her husband, Roy, and her daughters, Zoe and Irene.

Anita's website:
    http://www.anitamathias.com, and
Anita's blog Dreaming Beneath the Spires:
    http://dreamingbeneaththespires.blogspot.com

CPSIA information can be obtained
at www.ICGtesting.com
Printed in the USA
BVHW030917050222
627685BV00014B/4